Is it
really
green?

Is it *really* green?

Everyday eco dilemmas answered

Editors Megan Lea, Claire Cross
Designer Amy Child
Senior Editor Rona Skene
Project Art Editor Louise Brigenshaw
Jacket Designer Amy Cox
Jacket Coordinator Lucy Philpott
Pre-production Producer David Almond
Producer Francesca Sturiale
Creative Technical Support Sonia Charbonnier
Managing Editor Dawn Henderson
Managing Art Editor Marianne Markham
Art Director Maxine Pedliham
Publishing Director Katie Cowan

Illustrator Ana Karen Abitia Hill

First published in Great Britain in 2021
by Dorling Kindersley Limited
DK, One Embassy Gardens, 8 Viaduct Gardens,
London, SW11 7BW

The authorised representative in the EEA is
Dorling Kindersley Verlag GmbH. Arnulfstr. 124,
80636 Munich, Germany

Text copyright © 2021 Georgina Wilson-Powell
Copyright © 2021 Dorling Kindersley Limited
A Penguin Random House Company
10 9 8 7 6 5
006-318359-Jan/2021

A CIP catalogue record for this book is available from the British Library.
ISBN: 978-0-2414-3580-9

Printed and bound in Great Britain

For the curious
www.dk.com

RECYCLED
Paper made from
recycled material
FSC **FSC™ C018179**
www.fsc.org

This book was made with Forest Stewardship Council™ certified
paper – one small step in DK's commitment to a sustainable future.
For more information go to www.dk.com/our-green-pledge

CONTENTS

FOREWORD

Let's get this straight from the off. I'm like you. As much as I wish that I grew up on an organic farm, growing veg, I didn't. I had the normal childhood of a kid born in the '80s, replete with microwave chips, plastic-filled parties, and high-street fashion. No one ever gave a thought to what happened to the vast amount we consumed, day in, day out, beyond the bin.

When I was a teenager, most mainstream environmental campaigns focused on acid rain and saving the rainforests. "Global warming" felt theoretical at best; someone else's problem at worst. The trouble is it's not either of those. It's real, and it's here, affecting us through extreme weather events whether we care to acknowledge it or not. Sticking our fingers in our ears isn't an option: we all have a part to play.

While the Covid-19 pandemic has been a wake-up call for some, making us more thoughtful about what we buy, who we buy it from, and whether we need to buy at all, overconsumption remains our society's overriding issue. Our consumer power and desire for

stuff, experiences, and pleasure enable corporations to continue abusing the planet's resources, with disastrous results.

This book covers eco-dilemmas that I, and friends, colleagues and readers, have come up against in day-to-day life. Faced with confusing and often contradictory advice, it's easy to shrug and do nothing. Most of us are guilty; me included. That's the behaviour we need to change. I've tried to find the greenest, simplest solution in each case, or, if that is not possible, I've explained why.

Entire books could be written about each of the issues I touch on, but I wanted this to be dip-in-able, and to give you some straightforward tools to make changes at home, at work, and in your social networks; it's our everyday behaviours that we need to adapt.

So why am I the one writing this? Ten years ago, I found myself working in Dubai as a travel-magazine editor, experiencing the kind of jet-set lifestyle I could once have only dreamed of. As fun as it was,

I had the creeping sensation that the carbon footprint of my 25+ flights a year wasn't helping anyone, and it wasn't fulfilling me either. I became concerned about how unviable our beautiful world was becoming when I alone was getting through a small mountain of plastic water bottles per week and treated planes like buses.

None of us were born knowing what to do; we've had to learn, often going against behaviours ingrained in our upbringing. While most of us have financial limits, and we're all short of time, we can still make changes. If I can do it, so can you.

After I left Dubai, I wanted to do something that showcased the people who are finding new ways to combat the climate crisis, from making leather from apple skins to building boats that collect marine plastic. In 2016 I set up pebble, a free digital magazine for stylish, sustainable living.

Going green means making small changes that build into big shifts in social behaviour – look at how quickly we collectively ditched unnecessary plastic straws, or paused our travel in lockdown. Together we can exert pressure on those above us, be they global brands or governments. Don't despair, and don't give up. Use this book to establish quick wins and long-term goals. Share your progress, inspire your friends, talk to your boss or colleagues, ask questions, and don't give your money to people who don't share your concern about the climate emergency. Everyone can do something. The world needs you to start, in some way, today.

Georgina Wilson-Powell

So, is this book green?

We wanted to make this book in the least environmentally impactful way we could. We looked at each physical component of the book and examined where it came from and what it was made of; we found ways to limit the impact of transportation; and we took up greener habits in our workplaces. All of these principles are part of DK's Green Pledge, through which we aim to create and maintain a truly ethical supply chain. Here's our story.

The paper

We chose to use FSC-certified recycled paper, rather than "virgin" paper. Although using virgin paper means cutting down trees, it can be more environmentally friendly than certain recycled papers, due to the huge variation in the carbon footprints of suppliers. The Forest Stewardship Council (FSC) chain of custody certification provides credible assurance that the paper is sourced sustainably and ethically; we found two recycled-paper suppliers with strong histories of sustainable practices, ensuring that the paper

would have a relatively low carbon impact and not have to travel too far to the printers. We also chose lightweight paper, reducing the amount of raw materials required. Book covers are often coated in a plastic film to give a tactile finish and protect them from wear; we chose a water-based varnish instead, avoiding plastic and reducing energy use during the manufacturing process.

The ink

We used vegetable-oil-based rather than mineral-oil-based inks, as they are from renewable sources. We also decided to print in black and white instead of colour. While the quantity of ink used in each scenario would not differ significantly, using coloured ink requires more energy during printing.

The format

The choice between paperback and hardback was easy – the simpler binding process used for paperback books requires less energy and fewer materials. The book's size also matters: some formats result in more paper waste than others when the pages are trimmed from the printer's standard sheets of paper. The size we chose minimized this waste.

The printer

The location of the paper mills, printers, and warehouses all had to be taken into account. Keeping in mind the relative green credentials of different printers and the printing presses they use, and aiming to reduce the energy required for transportation, we printed as locally as we could to the mills and to each area in which we are selling the book – for example, printing the UK edition in the south of England, and the US and Canadian editions in eastern Canada. The printers we chose hold both ISO14001 and the FSC chain of custody certifications, both of which actively demonstrate verifiable commitment to sustainability.

Our way of working

We kept printing to a minimum while working on the book, sharing work digitally instead. We chose not to print proof copies for publicity purposes. We held meetings with external colleagues by video link, rather than asking them to travel into the office – and, once the country went into lockdown in early 2020, all meetings went digital. These tweaks to our ways of working have influenced our approach to every book we create.

Why not an e-book?

We want the information in this book to reach as many people as possible, which means producing both physical and digital copies. Studies suggest that you would need to read around 25 e-books a year for the energy and materials used to produce the e-reader to have less environmental impact than the same number of printed books. We encourage you to pass this book on to your friends and family once you have read it, and, eventually, to recycle it.

The climate emergency is real

Our world is at the brink of ecological collapse, which threatens all of humankind. We use the phrase "climate emergency" because it *is* an emergency. According to the United Nations, we had 11 years left to save the planet in 2019. This means we had 11 years to get our carbon emissions under control and keep our global temperature from rising by more than 1.5°C above pre-industrial levels. Otherwise, we risk experiencing a 3–4°C rise by 2100. That would threaten the abilities of our ecosystems and human societies to operate; it would cause our planet to become inhospitable and unrecognizable.

Our planet can only support the life that's on it when it's at the right temperature. A warmer world would mean, for starters, no ice caps. If all the ice sheets and glaciers on Earth melted, sea levels would rise by up to 60 metres, flooding coastal cities, farmland, and islands, causing large-scale migration inland. Even with the increase in temperature we've already experienced – of 1.1°C – the effects are clear. Sea levels have risen by 15cm. Extreme weather events have become more common (whether it's floods in the UK or wildfires in Australia), the seas are warming (which enables more extreme storms and threatens the

world's coral reefs), and we're losing key wildlife species at a dramatic rate. All of these issues have direct and indirect consequences, from food shortages to water scarcity, that compound and exacerbate one another.

How did this happen?

We didn't get here overnight. For decades, scientists have been warning of the unintended consequences of our reliance on practices that increase the amount of carbon in our atmosphere, such as the burning of fossil fuels and industrial agriculture. The latter arguably had a role to play

---

GLOBAL **CARBON EMISSIONS** HAVE INCREASED BY

640% SINCE THE 1950S

---

in the Covid-19 pandemic, which can be seen as a precursor to the climate-related emergencies we will experience in future if we don't adopt more sustainable agricultural practices.

Over the last 70 years, global temperatures have increased almost continuously. We're in this situation because of an unbridled lust for products and experiences that depend on finite resources, and a disconnection from the natural world, of which we are only a small part.

The climate emergency is also the perfect storm of conditions for us to not take action. It's often intangible, but it is changing landscapes and destroying lives at an accelerating pace. The problem is so enormous and complex that it has felt easier to wait for someone else to solve it. Governments, companies, and many individuals have ignored both natural warnings and those from experts, perhaps because change seemed too difficult, too big, or too unprofitable.

For many of us, the pandemic presented a breakdown of ordinary life that had previously been hard to imagine. The whole world has learnt lessons from the events of 2020, about both what to do and what not to do. Resilience and preparedness in the face of disaster are as important to surviving the climate crisis as reducing our carbon emissions.

The world is warmer now than it has ever been in the last 2,000 years. In 2021, there is no other way to look at the situation than as an emergency that affects everyone on Earth, and every generation to come.

Nine big problems facing our planet

Our world is a complex, interconnected place. When people talk about "climate change" they're often referring to one or more of the below issues, which all impact and affect each other.

1. Global warming

Global warming is due to the increase in greenhouse gases (water vapour, carbon dioxide, methane, nitrous oxide, fluorinated gases, and ozone) in the atmosphere, so called because they create a "greenhouse" effect. Heat from the sun is absorbed by the Earth's surface and radiated back out, but some of it is trapped by the greenhouse gases, making the surface of the Earth warmer than it would otherwise be. Our atmosphere keeps the planet at a habitable temperature, while protecting us from the most harmful of the sun's rays – but as we fill the air with more greenhouse gases from industrial activity, we increase its temperature. A warmer Earth disrupts weather patterns and threatens the survival of species all over the world.

2. Deforestation

Forests currently cover around 30% of the Earth's land area, but they are disappearing fast. Worldwide, we lose an area of ancient woodland equivalent in size to the UK every year. In the last 50 years, 17% of the Amazon rainforest has been cut down. As well as destroying the habitats of endangered animals and displacing indigenous peoples, deforestation has a profound effect on the climate. Trees act as "carbon sinks", absorbing CO_2 from the atmosphere and holding onto it for decades or centuries. They also protect biodiversity, prevent flooding and landslides, and even improve our mental health when we spend time walking among them. They're too precious to be chopped down en masse by corporations looking to plant more "valuable" crops (such as soya or cotton). And simply planting new trees isn't the answer: it would take decades for them to become as effective at storing carbon as the diverse ecosystems of rainforest or mangroves that are being lost.

3. Water security

According to the United Nations, rising temperatures, desertification, and industrial pollution are leading to the crisis-in-waiting of running out of clean water. A third of our groundwater systems are already in distress, as we're using up more fresh water than is being naturally replaced. In many parts of the world – often those that are already arid – freshwater systems aren't there when we need them.

Some lakes and rivers are drying up as weather patterns change, while other areas are regularly flooded. This imbalance, coupled with rising temperatures, will cause mass migration and geographical tensions over the next few decades.

4. Pollution

From toxic air to murky, poisoned rivers and dead-water zones caused by the fashion and farming industries, pollution is arguably the most visible effect of the climate emergency. The air in some cities and industrial areas is barely breathable, expanses of soil have been stripped of nutrients by industrial chemicals, and oil spills choke the seas. Pollution is killing landscapes, animals, and humans as well: air pollution is the fifth biggest risk factor for death globally and is thought to reduce lifespans by up to 10 years in the world's most polluted cities.

5. Waste

The more stuff we consume, the more we throw away. Most waste now contains plastic, which means it does not decompose or biodegrade; instead, it either collects in landfill and oceans or is burnt, adding to our air-pollution problem. It's thought that the equivalent of a truckload of plastic is dumped into our seas every minute. "Out of

▲ Many of the natural resources we rely on to live – such as land, water, fuel, and minerals – are being depleted at increasing rates due to overconsumption.

sight, out of mind" doesn't mean it has gone away: in fact, every piece of plastic ever produced still exists, and 90% of it has not been recycled. Many other environmental issues are linked to our cavalier attitude to waste. Food waste, for instance, is an enormous problem, and the intensely wasteful practices of the fashion industry are a huge drain on resources.

6. Biodiversity

Biodiversity (the array of different species of life forms and the web of connections between them) is essential for life on Earth. Each species has a role to play in keeping its natural environment flourishing, from pollinating crops to keeping food chains balanced by acting as predator or prey, to recycling organic waste. We need healthy forests to help us breathe clean air; we need crops to be pollinated to provide food; we need clean seas for healthy fish populations. Biodiversity is key to all of this. We're only just beginning to understand the complexity of our dependence on biodiversity; meanwhile, anywhere between 200 and 2,000 species become extinct per year. Globally, insect species have declined by 41% over the last four decades. One million plant and animal species are currently under threat of extinction.

▲ Climate scientists predict that, unless we make drastic changes to lifestyles in the developed world by the year 2030, the environment will be damaged beyond repair.

7. Ocean acidification

While ocean plastic gets a lot of media coverage, acidification is arguably a bigger killer. Marine life is possible thanks to a delicate balance of temperature and acidity. Our

---

OCEANS ABSORB AN ESTIMATED **93%** OF THE EXTRA HEAT CAUSED BY **GLOBAL WARMING**

---

oceans act like a sponge, absorbing CO_2 from the air. That CO_2 then mixes with water to form carbonic acid. The more CO_2 we emit, the more acidic the ocean becomes – 30% more, in fact, over the last 150 years. The result is an upset in the delicate balance of coral and other marine ecosystems, which can't survive. Dead zones, where no marine life can exist because of rising acidity or a lack of oxygen, are becoming more prevalent, and we're facing a loss of all of the world's coral reefs over the next few decades.

8. Soil erosion

Our humble soil does not get enough attention. What goes on beneath our feet and in our fields is incredibly important. Not only does healthy soil grow nutritious food, it also locks in three times more carbon than is in our atmosphere, prevents flooding, and cleans rainwater as it permeates through underground freshwater systems. Overfarming, monocrops, and widespread pesticide use have done enormous damage to this basic building block over the last century, creating depleted, lifeless soil that can't function properly. Organic, regenerative, and permaculture farming put restoring soil health at the heart of their practices.

9. Dwindling resources

All of the above issues put enormous pressure on resources such as land, water, and energy supplies, all of which we'll need more of if we hope to sustain our human population as it continues to grow. Barren oceans and land, as well as extreme weather events, make it harder to produce enough food to go round. We live on a finite planet, with finite resources, and yet expect infinite growth. It's thought that we will reach a point at which oil production levels can't be sustained within the next 60 years. As resources dwindle, they will become more expensive, utterly changing how we live.

We all have a part to play

Whether young or old, living in the UK or the UAE, you can create a positive impact. As consumers, the power is in our pockets. Every time you spend money, you vote for the future you want to see. Global brands might seem like they're in charge, but their success depends on your support. Choose where your hard-earned money goes and spend it consciously, on products that put the planet (and people) first. When we all decide to act, we can make changes much more quickly than we think – something that has been seen in every country during the Covid-19 pandemic. While "normal life" might not have returned yet, there has been a worldwide wake-up call to the fact that we can make widespread systematic changes within weeks; 2020 proved that it is possible to reshape and reorder our societies and global supply chains. We need to harness some of the willpower found during the pandemic in dealing with what will ultimately be a much longer-lasting global event.

It can feel overwhelming not knowing where to start, wondering if it really makes a difference what you

do, but use those feelings to fuel "active hope" – sitting and waiting is not the answer. Doing something feels better than doing nothing, every time. Focus on what's in front of you, doing what you can every day. Investing time and money in our local communities creates more resilient societies and supply chains, so let's apply that to the challenges ahead with our changing climate.

You don't have to label yourself an activist to make changes like the ones in this book. Even if your motivation is to save money (there's nothing wrong with that), the outcome is the same – helping to safeguard our planet. You don't live in a vacuum, either. Talk to your friends, family, and colleagues about the changes you're making, and why. Create or join new communities focused on the causes you're passionate about, whether at school, university, or your workplace, or through friend networks and family groups.

You can't solve everything, so pick something. Be kind. Be brave. Be bold. Our planet needs you.

GREEN
KITCHEN

Should I use a gas or electric hob and oven?

The "gas, electric, or induction" debate is something many cooks have strong opinions about. Luckily, the best option for the environment is easy to identify.

Gas hobs provide instant heat, but using a fossil fuel for cooking is not eco-friendly. Electric hobs can be powered by renewables, and, even though they take time to heat up, are more energy-efficient than gas. But for the most environmentally friendly hobs, induction is the way to go, as it is more energy-efficient than both gas and standard electric hobs. Bear in mind, however, that induction hobs use an electro-magnetic field to generate heat, which means that they won't work with pans made of copper or aluminium – you'll need pans made of magnetic metal, such as cast iron or stainless steel. Using a lid, matching ring size to pans, and shortcuts such as pre-boiling water in the kettle all speed up cooking times, reducing energy consumption regardless of hob type.

The greenest ovens are fan-assisted. They use around 20% less energy than regular ovens, because they warm up more quickly.

Other eco-friendly cooking hacks include choosing the toaster over the grill where possible, and using a slow cooker for stews and similar dishes, as these use less power than an oven.

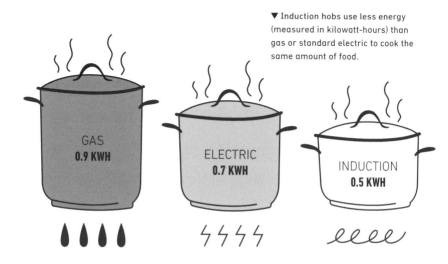

▼ Induction hobs use less energy (measured in kilowatt-hours) than gas or standard electric to cook the same amount of food.

GAS
0.9 KWH

ELECTRIC
0.7 KWH

INDUCTION
0.5 KWH

How can I make sure my fridge and freezer are as green as they can be?

Fridges and freezers are essential items in any kitchen, but they can be energy guzzlers. There are a few things you can do to minimize their eco-impact.

Because they are large home appliances that are switched on all the time, your fridge and freezer can use up a lot of energy. Their efficiency depends on a number of factors.

When fridges and freezers are positioned near appliances that give off heat, such as an oven, washing machine, or dishwasher, or are in direct sunlight, they have to work harder to stay cold, using more energy. Fridges and freezers release their heat via condenser coils, which are either at the base or, particularly on older models, at the back. If there is no gap between the back of the fridge and the wall, or if the condenser coils are dusty, it can't release heat as easily, so again has to work harder.

The eco-impact doesn't end there. While the use of ozone-layer-destroying chlorofluorocarbons (CFCs) as the coolant in fridges has long been outlawed, some countries, including the US, still use the substitutes hydrofluorocarbons (HFCs), and hydrochlorofluorocarbons (HCFCs). The release of these potent greenhouse gases into the atmosphere when fridges are disposed of has contributed to global warming.

Here's how to minimize the eco-impact of your fridge or freezer:

- **If you're planning** a new kitchen layout, place the fridge and freezer away from heat sources.
- **If you're looking** for a new fridge, choose one with an energy-efficiency rating of A or above, and

---

3.5 million
FRIDGES ARE THROWN AWAY **EACH YEAR** IN THE UK

---

don't go overboard on size. A bigger model will take more energy to run, so don't be tempted to buy a larger one than you actually need.

- **Maintenance** is also key: make sure the rubber seals around the door are in good working order: if cool air can leak out, your fridge or freezer will be less efficient. Dust the outside of the condenser coils a couple of times a year.
- **Keep the thermostat** at the recommended temperature for chilled or frozen foods. Too cold and you'll waste energy; too warm and you'll end up wasting food.

Is it worth washing up a yogurt pot before recycling it?

Rinsing out your empty food containers before putting them in the bin might seem like a waste of water, but it can be key to keeping the recycling system running efficiently.

The answers to this dilemma, though straightforward, differ depending on where you live. You need to rinse glass, metal, and plastic containers and packaging clean if you're recycling in the UK or US. In the UK, recycling goes to materials recovery facilities to be processed, and if any of the items in a bin are contaminated, the entire load is at risk of not being able to be sorted and recycled. And yes, food waste counts as contamination. If they can't be recycled, the items are burnt or go to landfill, making the whole system wasteful. So if you live somewhere where rinsing your yogurt pots and pasta-sauce jars is a requirement, do so with pride.

Recycling etiquette

It's the same issue if you muddle up your recycling, or put items that can't be recycled, such as black plastic cartons and most pizza boxes, into recycling bins. It runs the risk of derailing the whole load.

While rinsing items uses water, it saves the wasted energy of a recycling system that isn't recycling (which also costs you money in taxes). In some countries, such as Australia, there's no need to rinse items yourself, as they can be cleaned at the recycling facilities. Do your research before taking any chances.

The real debate is how much rubbish is actually recycled. Several countries that were once thought of as among the world's best recyclers actually send a lot of their recycling abroad, where it's often dumped or burnt (see p.24).

- **Get familiar** with your area's recycling policy by looking online or contacting your local authority.
- **Don't go overboard** washing up items – they don't need to be squeaky clean, just well-rinsed.
- **Greasy cardboard** (including pizza boxes), plastic bags, heat-resistant glass (such as Pyrex), and styrofoam are all big recycling no-nos, so don't be tempted to try.

25% ON AVERAGE OF MATERIALS SENT TO RECYCLING **ARE** CONTAMINATED

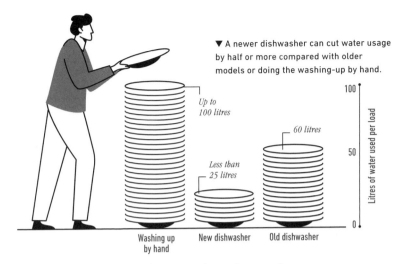

▼ A newer dishwasher can cut water usage by half or more compared with older models or doing the washing-up by hand.

Up to 100 litres

60 litres

Less than 25 litres

Litres of water used per load

100

50

0

Washing up by hand | New dishwasher | Old dishwasher

Should I wash up by hand or use the dishwasher?

Energy-efficient dishwashers have come a long way. Use it wisely, and this kitchen convenience can become an eco-warrior, cutting down on water waste.

Modern dishwashers are less wasteful than you might think. They do a full load using a fraction of the water that you'd need to wash the same number of dishes by hand at the sink. A fast-running tap can shoot out 9 litres of water a minute; a dishwasher might use 25 litres per load.

Both options use a similar amount of energy, but when you take into account the extra water that washing up uses, dishwashers have the edge. There are a few caveats, though: only run it on full, use the eco setting (which saves up to 20% of electricity), and scrape rather than rinse leftovers from the dishes first – if you pre-rinse your dishes, you could be wasting up to 27,000 litres of water a year. Finally, skip the dry cycle, leaving the door open to let the dishes dry instead.

While a dishwasher is relatively environmentally friendly wash-by-wash, that doesn't take into account its manufacture and disposal. Choose the most energy-efficient model you can afford, and maintain it (cleaning filters, removing residue, and so on) to extend its life. If you don't have a dishwasher, use as little water as you can when washing up, by not leaving the tap running.

How much of what we throw away is actually recycled?

It's great to make the effort to recycle, but what happens once it's out of our sight? The system isn't always as green as we might hope.

Our eco mantra is "reduce, reuse, recycle", and there's a reason why "recycle" comes last. Dealing with the mountain of recycling waste we generate is a challenge; how much of your recycling waste is processed is totally dependent on where you live.

In many countries, the waste from your recycling bin is sent first to materials recovery facilities, where cardboard, aluminium, plastic, and so on are sorted. Most of this is then traded overseas, usually to Asia. China stopped accepting other countries' waste in 2018, a change that has led to some developing nations becoming the world's "bin". What happens to recycling waste in these countries is unclear. Glass and metal are cleaned and melted into new materials, but other materials are often buried, or else they are burnt, releasing toxic emissions.

Rich countries tend to produce a lot of waste: in the US, for instance, the average person generates 2kg a day. The EU aimed to get each country recycling at least 50% of household

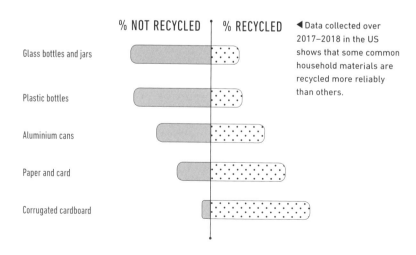

% NOT RECYCLED | **% RECYCLED**

Glass bottles and jars

Plastic bottles

Aluminium cans

Paper and card

Corrugated cardboard

◀ Data collected over 2017–2018 in the US shows that some common household materials are recycled more reliably than others.

waste by 2020, but only a few countries achieved this. Globally, we recycle only around 9% of plastics.

It's difficult to feel empowered in this situation, especially when the authorities are failing to lead. We need openness and simpler systems so we know what can and can't be recycled. In countries such as Germany, Sweden, Luxembourg,

---

40% OF ALL THE UK'S RUBBISH, INCLUDING RECYCLING, ENDS UP BEING BURNT

---

and Ireland, clear instructions and demarcated bins have ensured efficient recycling.

To help reduce the waste burden:
- **Reframe how recycling** factors into your household waste stream: reduce consumption and reuse what you can to avoid producing waste in the first place.
- **Recycle wherever possible**. Plastic items have a numbering system that indicates whether or not they can be recycled: if it's a 2, 4, or 5 they can be recycled; otherwise, they can't.
- **Ask your local authority** where your recycling goes. Do the companies used have transparent and responsible waste-management policies? Consider campaigning for local change if not.

Is it worth separating food waste from regular waste?

An extra bin for food waste might seem like an inconvenience, but the planet will thank you.

One study in Australia reported that over 35% of the contents of the average household bin is made up of food waste.

It is definitely worth separating your food waste from general waste if you have a local food-recyling scheme or a compost bin at home. When food ends up in landfill it doesn't break down efficiently. Food waste requires light and oxygen to decompose, both of which are lacking in landfill. Instead, the food breaks down very slowly, and in the process releases methane, a potent greenhouse gas.
- **Aim to produce** as little food waste as possible in the first place (see p.26).
- **If your local authority** collects food waste for recycling, take full advantage. They may compost food waste for use as fertilizer (effectively "recycling" it) or turn it into fuel, which can produce heat or electricity, or power transport.
- **Alternatively, compost** your own food waste – see pp.160–61 for tips on how to do this.

How can I reduce and reuse food waste at home?

Food waste is a huge environmental issue. If you find yourself regularly throwing away food, there is almost certainly something you can do about it.

With an estimated one-third of the food produced globally going uneaten, the issue of food waste is of serious concern. Wasting food means wasting resources, including the energy and water that is used to produce and transport it. The amount of food that goes uneaten every year requires a land mass larger than China to grow. If food ends up rotting in landfill, rather than being composted or used for fuel (see p.25), it produces the potent greenhouse gas methane, contributing to global warming.

Reducing food waste

Planning what to buy, understanding how to store food so it lasts longer, and using up leftovers are all key to reducing waste.

- **Start a meal planner** to help you buy less and use up the ingredients you already have in your cupboard.

▼ A study of households in Ireland found that the majority of food thrown away could easily be saved from the bin.

60% AVOIDABLE
FOOD WASTE

20% POTENTIALLY
AVOIDABLE

20%
UNAVOIDABLE

- **Make a shopping list** from your meal planner and stick to it.
- **Be choosy about** the brands you buy, and be wary of special offers: "buy one, get one free" is designed to be tempting, but it's only worth it if you know you'll eat all of the food.

4.5 million
TONNES OF FOOD **IS WASTED** ANNUALLY IN THE UK

- **Learn how to** store fresh food. For instance, keep potatoes in dark cupboards, put mushrooms in the fridge inside a paper bag to stop them going slimy, and place fresh herbs in water in the fridge (apart from basil, which perishes if chilled).
- **Make good use** of the freezer. Freeze surplus fresh herbs or leftover wine (yes, really) in an ice-cube tray, to use as needed for cooking. Whizz up stale bread and freeze the breadcrumbs, and chop up and freeze surplus veg, so you have ready-to-go portions.
- **Use glass or plastic** containers to store dried goods, and label leftovers that you freeze, so you can keep stock of what you have.

Using up food

There are endless ways to be inventive in the kitchen. A little online research can yield dozens of simple recipe ideas, from rustling up a smoothie to blitzing avocado, beans, tomatoes, or beetroot into hummus. Get creative:

- **Use every part** of the foodstuffs you buy. Think herb stalks used for pesto, chicken bones for stock, or citrus rinds to flavour gin or vodka.
- **Bulk-cook stews**, veggie tagines, curries, and so on, to use up plentiful seasonal produce, then freeze the additional portions for later use.
- **Use leftovers** from your evening meal to make a delicious lunch the following day. It sounds obvious, but how often do you do it? This both cuts waste and removes the temptation to buy plastic-covered takeaway lunches. If you're taking your lunch to work, use airtight containers to transport food easily.

A zero-waste mindset

- **Do a food-waste audit**, assessing everything your household throws away in a week. Once you've got an idea of where your weak points are, set a challenge for the household to eliminate them.
- **Before throwing something** away, ask yourself: is there enough for another entire meal, or can I incorporate what's left into my next one? You'll get a real buzz when you manage to use up everything.

"Living more sustainably often means returning *to older, natural solutions.*"

What should I be washing up wit

If you're doing the dishes by hand, sponges, scourers, and dishcloths are essential, but unsustainable throwaway options are dirtying the planet.

We've washed dishes with blue-and-white woven cloths and green-and-yellow sponge-scourers for decades without thinking anything of it, but these items are actually harmful. Those sponges, made from polyurethane, don't last long in our kitchens but stick around in landfill for centuries. Short-lived woven cloths are mostly made from viscose (which is made of wood pulp in a chemical- and energy-heavy process), and, while they do biodegrade under the right conditions, the majority of them end up in landfill, where there's neither enough air nor heat for microbes to break them down.

The best renewable alternatives last for longer in the kitchen, and don't take years to decompose once thrown away. Swap packets of supermarket dishcloths for cut-up old bits of fabric, which can be boiled to get rid of bacteria, then reused. Choose wooden scrubbing brushes with bristles made from horsehair or cactus; scourers made of agave twine or copper wire (which can be recycled); and washing-up pads made of coconut fibre, loofah, or cellulose. Online stores and many zero-waste shops offer a wide range of options that don't hurt the environment and come in recyclable, plastic-free packaging.

▼ Comparing useful life and time taken to degrade once binned, natural options such as recycled cotton dishcloths come out on top.

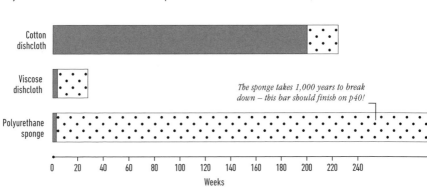

Useful life

Time to decompose

The sponge takes 1,000 years to break down – this bar should finish on p40!

Cotton dishcloth

Viscose dishcloth

Polyurethane sponge

0 20 40 60 80 100 120 140 160 180 200 220 240

Weeks

Which cleaning products should I avoid?

There are two reasons to avoid mainstream cleaning products: what's in them, and what they come in. Natural alternatives will help keep your conscience – as well as your home – clean.

Many of the chemicals found in cleaning products cause harm when they find their way into our soil, waterways, and oceans, and have an impact on our health. Avoid anything containing sodium hypochlorite (the active ingredient in bleach). When this chemical leaks into bodies of water, it can mix with other chemicals to create chlorine compounds, including dioxins, which are highly toxic to animals and humans and remain in the environment for long periods. Many cleaning products are also tested on animals, so always do your research before you buy.

200 DIFFERENT CHLORINE COMPOUNDS HAVE BEEN FOUND IN THE US'S GREAT LAKES

Once those plastic bottles containing cleaning products are empty, they'll be floating around the ocean or breaking down into microplastics for centuries. There are eco-friendly cleaning wipes that biodegrade within a year in a compost bin, but in general it's best to resist them. Most come in plastic packaging, and they're still a single-use, throwaway product.

You don't need bleach or scientific-sounding antibacterial products to get rid of limescale and stubborn stains – there are plenty of more Earth-friendly options that get the job done just as well:

- **Consider making** your own natural, low-tech cleaning products; look for traditional recipes that centre on white vinegar, lemon juice, and bicarbonate of soda.
- **If you buy, choose** plant-based cleaning products, available in supermarkets and online. Buy from companies that offer a refill service, which will also help reduce your single-use plastic consumption, or avoid containers altogether by using solid cleaning bars. Look for organic ingredients and a cruelty-free logo to ensure that your cleaning products are as planet-friendly as possible.

Should I use kitchen roll or washable alternatives?

Kitchen roll, a modern-day essential in many homes, might seem like a greener option than washing and rewashing tea towels, napkins, and cloths, but in fact the opposite is true.

The process of manufacturing kitchen roll is heavy on resources and energy: it takes 17 trees and 91,000 litres of water to make just one tonne; it is then infused with toxic chemicals to make it stronger, and bleached white. Each year we get through more than 6.5 million tonnes worldwide.

While washing tea towels, napkins, and cloths uses water and energy, the amounts needed are a fraction of those used to make the new kitchen roll you'd have to buy every week.

On top of that, reusable tea towels and cloths don't add to the demand for virgin materials, making them a more sustainable option long-term. A green kitchen means kicking kitchen roll to the kerb.

- **If you're shopping** for tea towels and napkins, choose natural fibres such as linen or organic cotton, as they don't contain chemicals or shed microplastics (see p.96).
- **To avoid buying** new cloths, cut old clothing into pieces. These can be washed with your laundry between uses. Scraps of fabric are ideal for mopping up spills and wiping down surfaces.
- **If you don't want** to move away from paper, switch to reusable bamboo paper towels: they are naturally antibacterial and can be washed several times. Fast-growing bamboo, when ethically sourced, is a renewable resource, and biodegrades quickly in compost.

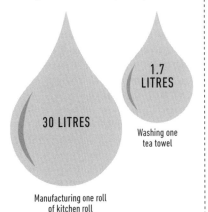

1.7 LITRES

Washing one tea towel

30 LITRES

Manufacturing one roll of kitchen roll

▲ It takes a lot more water to manufacture kitchen roll than to reuse and wash a tea towel – cutting back by one roll saves more than 28 litres of water.

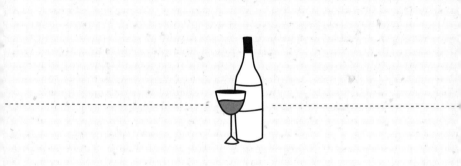

FOOD AND DRINK

Is a vegan diet always better for the environment?

Cutting out meat and dairy is generally lighter on the planet, but being vegan isn't without its own dilemmas. Your individual choices make a difference.

According to a 2019 paper from the Intergovernmental Panel on Climate Change (IPCC), our food-producing systems are responsible for up to 37% of our greenhouse-gas emissions. Globally, our ever-rising consumption of meat and dairy supports energy-intensive, industrial-scale farming practices. Together, meat and dairy production swallow up 77% of all agricultural land and account for 60% of agriculture's carbon emissions, yet these foods provide just 17% of the calories we eat. Furthermore, 33% of the agricultural land the meat and dairy industries utilize is used to grow feed for livestock – more than 70 billion animals are reared for food worldwide each year. In many countries, the large-scale rearing of animals for meat and dairy contributes to mass deforestation, as trees make way for more intensive, chemical-laden arable farming to feed the livestock. Turning plant food into meat instead of consuming it directly reduces its calorific value tenfold. Some studies suggest that eating a vegan diet can reduce your carbon "foodprint" by up to 73%.

However, being vegan isn't without a potential eco-impact. In the past few decades, the rise of "superfoods"

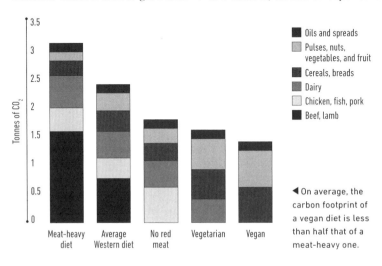

◀ On average, the carbon footprint of a vegan diet is less than half that of a meat-heavy one.

has led to an unprecedented demand for particular items. Avocados and almond milk are two examples where growing consumer demand has had dire regional impacts (see p.55 and p.42). Making any unsustainably produced food a staple of your diet is clearly unhelpful for the environment. In addition, the high-protein pulses upon which a vegan diet is heavily dependent are mainly grown in warm climates – transporting these foods around the world has a carbon cost.

Nonetheless, there is a clear consensus that a locally produced, seasonal, mostly plant-based diet is the greenest way to eat. This also means you are no longer associated with the animal cruelty that is commonplace in industrial farming.

Every meal we eat provides an opportunity to make eco-friendly choices for the planet. Eat greener by considering the following:

- **If you're not keen** to go fully vegan, a "flexitarian" approach can make a difference. Try eating plant-based a few days a week, or swapping to vegan for a percentage of your meals. If you do eat meat, make it an occasional treat, so you can spend a bit more on local, organically reared livestock.
- **Whether you're vegan** or not, aim to eat seasonally as much as possible. Research where your food comes from (see p.50) and avoid, or limit, foods that are unsustainably produced or need to be flown long distances to your table.

Can I eat dairy and eggs and still be green?

If you're not ready to go fully plant-based, it's worth looking at where you get your dairy products from.

Stopping your consumption of meat and fish withdraws support for the environmentally destructive meat industry and unsustainable fishing practices. However, the impact on the planet of the dairy industry also shouldn't be underestimated (see p.42). In the US, almost one-fifth of the agricultural water supply is used in rearing 9 million dairy cows; in the UK, a staggering 13 billion eggs are consumed in a year. In addition, the enormous farms that are often needed to supply these products gobble up huge amounts of power, animal feed, and antibiotics, with their associated air miles – representing millions of tonnes of greenhouse-gas emissions. Cutting out dairy and eggs helps to reduce demand for the damaging practices of intensive agricultural industries.

If you don't want to give up dairy and eggs altogether, consider cutting down your consumption, and buying local, organic, and free range when you do. If you have the space, you could even keep your own chickens!

Are some types of meat greener than others?

While eating meat is often viewed as categorically not green, not all meat is equal: it's possible to eat greener by making more considered choices about the sorts of meat you consume.

Mass-market meat that is exported around the world is undeniably hard on the planet, with a high cost in terms of greenhouse-gas emissions, deforestation to make way for livestock and grow their feed, and soil degradation caused by the waste from factory farms. What's more, the cramped conditions in industrial-scale farms ignore animal welfare. And the practice of routinely pumping livestock with antibiotics, used preventatively in healthy animals and, in some countries, as growth promoters, raises the threat of antibiotic resistance in humans.

Beef and lamb are the worst offenders when it comes to greenhouse gas emissions. Together, these two animals produce more methane than all other types of livestock combined.

Chicken has a relatively small carbon footprint, but often scores low on the welfare stakes. In the UK, for instance, most supermarket

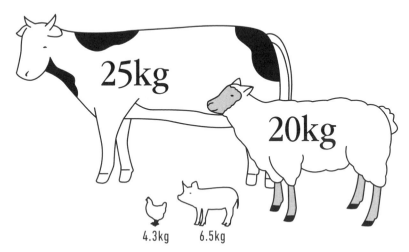

▲ The carbon footprints of livestock vary with farming practices, but here are the global averages, in kilograms of CO_2-equivalent emitted per 100g of protein.

chickens are the Ross variety. Alive for just 35 days, the chickens are forced to grow unnaturally quickly. Up to 50,000 birds can be crammed into a single shed, and kept awake with artificial light for long periods to speed up growth.

Greener options

There are other methods of keeping livestock that are less environmentally damaging, and can even have a positive effect. For instance, well-managed, grass-fed cattle can improve soil quality and sequester carbon, often on land that otherwise wouldn't be used. These practices aren't possible in all climates, however, and can't be done cheaply. This means that the impact of meat production varies enormously across different countries. For instance, beef in South America has, on average, three times the carbon footprint of beef in Europe.

Choosing more unusual types of meat can also be greener. Veal (meat from male calves) is a by-product of the dairy industry. It has been controversial due to its inhumane production method, but a new industry of ethically reared veal is emerging. The calves are often partly pasture-fed, and, because they consume less water and grain than full-grown beef cattle, and produce less methane, the meat is more sustainable than beef.

Native, lighter-footed animals (such as deer) that don't compact the soil as much as heavy cattle can also be more sustainable. Less compacted soil means more water absorption,

which helps mitigate the risk of flooding. Game (non-farmed meat, such as venison and wood pigeon) is often more sustainable than farmed meat, especially if it comes from animals that are culled to control their numbers, though the practice is in itself controversial.

There are also advances being made in the world of lab-grown meat. The idea is enticing from an animal-welfare point of view, but would only be less environmentally damaging than "real" meat if the labs' energy use could be minimized, and toxic by-products avoided.

To lessen your environmental impact while enjoying meat, aim to eat less, and better:

- **Cut down your consumption**. Eating less meat means you can spend more on sustainable, organic varieties when you do buy it.

- **Avoid cheap supermarket** meat and support local, sustainable, and/or organic farms. Here, animals roam freely outdoors on land that isn't over-farmed, and graze on grass, rather than being fed solely on grain.

- **Adopt the** "nose to tail" philosophy of eating meat, whereby each part, or as much as possible, of the animal is used. For instance, if you're cooking a roast chicken, use the carcass to make stock, which reduces waste and cuts back on the amount of other products you buy.

- **Once you've bought** meat, don't waste it. Explore recipes online for inventive ideas for leftovers.

"One in five millennials has changed their diet *to limit their environmental impact.*"

Can I eat fish without damaging the planet?

Eating fish is often seen as a healthy option for both our bodies and the environment, but unsustainable fishing practices put the eco-credentials of a pescatarian diet in doubt.

The complex marine ecosystems that once surrounded our coastlines have been decimated by commercial fishing. While fishing isn't necessarily damaging in itself, overfishing – when fish are caught faster than they can be replaced – is. Trawlers that use 120km-long nets and hooks to dredge vast expanses of the seabed wreak havoc on ecosystems. Overfishing is the biggest threat to our sea life, beyond even plastic (microplastics are now found in most fish and shellfish) and other pollutants, and is rapidly pushing fish stocks to the point of extinction.

Farmed fish fare little better. Over-crowding in intensive farms encourages disease and parasites such as sea lice. To counter this, fish are given antibiotics, and pesticides are pumped into the water. This damages the surrounding environment, degrading habitats and marine biodiversity.

When buying fish:

- **Check for certification** on supermarket fish signalling that it was sustainably sourced. In the UK, the Marine Conservation Society (MCS) traffic light system ranks fish from most to least sustainable, and a "blue tick" logo shows that fisheries have been independently audited by the Marine Stewardship Council (MSC). Research the stock levels of the types of fish on sale, and don't buy anything that's endangered.

- **If you're close** to the coast, buy from local fishermen or fishmongers, so you can check how the fish were caught.

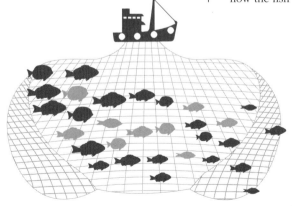

Illegal catch
Legal catch

◀ An estimated 30% of fish sold as food are caught illegally, causing fish stocks to fall to dangerously low levels.

What is the environmental impact of soya?

Industrial-scale farming of soya has led to alarming rates of deforestation. Knowing where the soya we buy comes from and how it is used is key to a more sustainable approach.

In the past 20 years the demand for soya has rocketed, with a resulting 400% increase in its production. While its growing popularity may be partly due to more people eating plant-based diets, the vast majority of soya beans don't end up as food for humans. They are used to feed industrially farmed cows, pigs, chickens, and other livestock.

How is soya grown?

Most of the soya we use comes from Brazil, where its production has contributed to deforestation.

Since 2006, many countries have committed to not buying soya grown on former Amazonian rainforest land. However, many soya farmers in the region have simply turned to other ancient forests, such as the Brazilian Cerrado, instead. The decimation of these forests has led to soil degradation, increased flooding and mudslides, and the loss of precious wildlife habitats.

In addition, soya is grown as a "monocrop", or "monoculture", a single crop species occupying a large area of land. As well as degrading

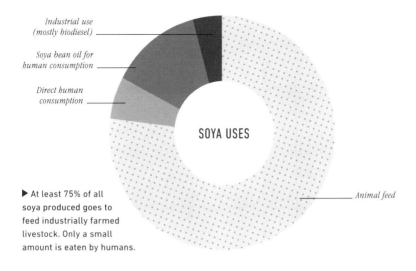

Industrial use (mostly biodiesel)

Soya bean oil for human consumption

Direct human consumption

SOYA USES

Animal feed

▶ At least 75% of all soya produced goes to feed industrially farmed livestock. Only a small amount is eaten by humans.

soil, this industrial-scale production uses up unsustainable amounts of water, energy, and chemicals, and renders the crop highly susceptible to pests and diseases. The intensive use of fertilizers and pesticides, kills off insects, poisons rivers, and creates toxic soil that is unable to nourish other plants.

To make it easier to manage, most soya is genetically modified (GM), which means that the crop's DNA

HALVING **EUROPE'S MEAT CONSUMPTION** WOULD **CUT SOYMEAL USE** BY **75%**

---

has been engineered to give it specific properties. GM soya is made resistant to strong herbicides for easy weed control; as the weeds become resistant to the chemicals sprayed on them, farmers use stronger chemicals, compounding environmental problems such as water eutrophication and acidification of soil and waterways.

Greener alternatives

Sustainably grown soya does exist, but many charities and NGOs cast doubt on just how green the ratings are. As with many food-related issues, there's no easy solution to the problems raised by large-scale soya production. Research is being done

into alternatives – for instance, feeding livestock with insects instead of soymeal could be a significant step towards making animal products greener.

The most effective way to shrink the current demand for soya is to curb our consumption of grain-fed meat. Here's how to reduce your soya footprint:

- **Aim to source** locally reared meat that comes from grass-fed rather than grain-fed livestock. Generally, these animals will have enjoyed a life outside, as opposed to the industrial systems more usually associated with grain-fed meat. Grass-fed meat also tends to be higher in nutrients.
- **Check out the provenance** of soya products. If possible, check the country of origin to ensure that the soya was not grown in a rainforest zone and that it comes from a plantation that follows a crop-rotation system, commits to not damaging the landscape, and pledges to preserve biodiversity.
- **If buying tofu products,** choose organic whenever possible, to be sure of avoiding chemical nasties. Some people have concerns that tofu simply labelled "natural" may have been processed with hexane, a liquid produced from refining crude oil; studies have found that hexane can cause brain damage in rats.

Which milk alternative is the greenest?

There is an abundance of dairy-free milks out there, but within the range of plant-based alternatives, some options are definitely greener than others.

It's estimated that the dairy industry is responsible for around 3–4% of global greenhouse-gas emissions. Growing grain to feed dairy cows requires a great deal of land, much of which could otherwise be used to grow crops to feed the world's human population. Industrial-scale dairy farming also contributes to deforestation and biodiversity loss, as well as soil degradation and eutrophication of waterways, thanks to the huge quantities of chemical-laden waste produced. What's more, dairy cows on large farms often lead miserable lives, with newborns separated from mothers, male calves culled, and cows over-milked to exhaustion. The green argument for switching to vegan milks is clear.

Comparing plant milks

As with all environmental lifestyle swaps, it pays to check out the green credentials of the various alternatives before you make the leap:

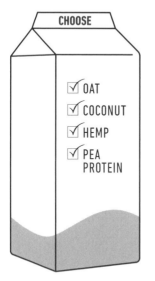

CHOOSE

☑ OAT
☑ COCONUT
☑ HEMP
☑ PEA PROTEIN

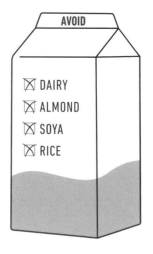

AVOID

☒ DAIRY
☒ ALMOND
☒ SOYA
☒ RICE

▲ Nutritional benefits aside, the "milks" listed on the left carton are usually greener choices than those on the right.

- **Oat** milk stands out as one of the most eco-friendly plant milks. Oats tend not to be intensively farmed, are responsible for relatively low CO_2 emissions, and use six times less water than almonds to grow (see below). In addition, the waste from their production can be used as a biogas, though not all brands do this. Oats can also be grown in cooler northern climes, where plant milks are especially popular, meaning fewer air miles between farm and consumer.

- **Coconut** milk is also a good choice. It may need to travel further to many of the markets where demand is high, but coconuts need little water or chemicals to grow, and the trees are good carbon sinks, absorbing CO_2 throughout their lives.

- **Hemp** milk, made from the seeds of the hemp plant, is full of protein and fatty acids. The hardy plant flourishes in most places without the aid of pesticides and using relatively little water. Every part of the plant can be used, so there is little waste.

- **Pea-protein** milk, made from yellow split peas, uses 25 times less water to produce than cow's milk and 100 times less than almond milk. Nutritionally it scores well, too, being high in protein and calcium.

- **Almonds** have had a popularity explosion in recent years, as their health benefits have been lauded by experts and bloggers. The resulting global demand has placed a huge strain on the US state of California, where most large almond farms are, and where climate change has already led to almost permanent drought. Like most tree crops, almonds must be watered year-round, so growers are forced to divert water from elsewhere to irrigate them, putting the state's future water supply in jeopardy. In addition, the pesticides used on almond trees pose a risk to the bees that pollinate them. In 2018–19 alone, over 50 billion bees were wiped out in the almond industry. Other nut milks can be sourced

IT TAKES OVER **3 litres** OF WATER TO GROW A **SINGLE ALMOND**

from non-drought areas; choose responsible brands, or try making your own nut milk at home.

- **Soya** milk is associated with the unsustainable practices of industrial soya farming (see p.40), so many mainstream brands may not be green. However, this isn't true of all soya production – so, again, do your research before you buy.

- **Rice** is a water-intensive crop, and may also have been genetically modified (see p.41). Rice fields also release large amounts of the greenhouse gases methane and nitrous oxide as the rice grows.

Should I always avoid items that contain palm oil?

The palm oil debate is more complicated than you might think. Avoiding palm oil is a good start, but understanding the impact of alternative products is equally important.

Palm oil – an edible oil produced by crushing the fruit of oil palm trees – is everywhere. It's used in a range of different processed foods, from sweets to ready meals (where it improves shelf life and texture), and is also found in skincare products, makeup, and many other everyday goods. It appears under hundreds of pseudonyms, so you might not always recognize it at first glance.

Around 85% of the world's palm oil is produced in Malaysia and Indonesia. As a quick cash crop, oil palms are grown on such a large scale that their production has destroyed ancient jungles, displaced indigenous people, and endangered wildlife. Oil palms are also grown on large areas of peatland, where drainage for cultivation not only degrades the land but also releases huge amounts of CO_2.

Unfortunately, the solution is not as simple as just switching to different oils. Other vegetable oils, such as sunflower oil and coconut oil, are much less efficient to grow than palm oil, with crop yields up to ten times lower. Satisfying the current demand with less space-efficient crops would mean damaging even more land.

Things get even more complicated when you consider sustainably sourced palm oil. This is produced from plantations verified by a global accreditation scheme, the Roundtable on Sustainable Palm Oil (RSPO). Some see it as an acceptable option, as fewer pesticides are used in its

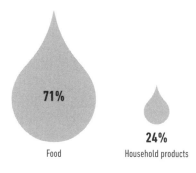

71%
Food

24%
Household products

5%
Biofuels

◀ Most of the palm oil produced globally is used in food, including snack foods such as chocolate and crisps, as well as bread and ready meals.

production than for regular palm oil. Others, including Greenpeace and the World Wide Fund for Nature (WWF), say that the sustainable credentials aren't high enough and that too much wildlife and land is still being abused. In this instance, there really isn't a viable eco-friendly alternative yet.

It's a difficult situation, but there are ways to be greener:

- **Try to reduce** your consumption of the sorts of products that use palm oil. Our demand for convenient, processed foods has rocketed over the last 50 years; to really solve the palm-oil problem we need to reduce that demand.

PALM OIL IS IN NEARLY **50%** OF **PRODUCTS IN SUPERMARKETS**

Swapping to products that contain alternative, sustainably sourced oils is a good idea in the short term, but moving away from processed foods (and mainstream skincare – see p.80) altogether is the greener goal.

- **Get to know** palm oil's aliases: "palm kernel oil", "palmolein", "glyceryl", and "stearate" are the most common.
- **Download** one of the apps available that allow you to scan products in supermarkets to find out if they contain palm oil.

Which is the greenest cooking oil?

What matters more than the type of oil you go for is how and where it was produced.

Mass-producing any oil has a negative impact on the land, through chemical use, deforestation, or biodiversity loss. On top of that, each oil-producing crop has its own issues. For instance, olive-oil producers are dealing with a disease that is killing their ancient trees, which will cause the price of olive oil to rise, while many coconut farmers in Asia live in poverty (despite the boom in demand for coconut oil), due to unfair business practices.

Here's what to think about when choosing cooking oils:

- **Opt for organic** oils if you can.
- **If possible, buy oils** that haven't travelled long distances to get to you, such as rapeseed oil if you live in the UK. A glut of a particular oil crop in the country where you live provides a great opportunity to buy local.
- **Look for Fairtrade** products, or another certification that ensures the farmers and crop pickers were paid and treated fairly.
- **Avoid plastic bottles** and choose glass instead. You can also look for opportunities to refill your oil bottle at a local zero-waste shop (see p.115), or buy oil in bulk.

Is it really greener to eat organic?

Organic farming sounds like an obvious green win, but it's been the subject of fierce debate, with some detractors raising issues concerning the practice's land use.

Organic food production aims to grow food naturally, without artificial interventions. This means avoiding the use of synthetic chemicals to kill pests and weeds or increase the yield of crops, as well as steering clear of genetic modification (GM), the practice of altering the genetic make-up of crops (see p.41 for more on this). There are different organic standards across the world, which is one reason why certification is so confusing. For instance, some organic farmers use pesticides (more on that below).

The importance of soil

Key to the organic–non-organic debate is soil. Conventional, chemical-laden farming degrades soil both through overusing it to grow the same crops in one area continually (known as monoculture), and through introducing chemicals in the form of pesticides and fertilizers. This has several effects. When the soil's balance of nutrients and physical structure changes, the insects, worms, and microbes that live in it can no longer survive, affecting the local ecosystem and disrupting food chains. In addition, overworking, or eroding, the top layer of soil diminishes its ability to store carbon (see pp.208–209) and absorb rainwater, making it a less effective barrier against both global warming and flooding.

Organic farming helps restore and retain soil health, improving biodiversity and allowing our soil to remain an effective carbon sink.

Room for improvement

One downside to organic farming is its efficiency. Organic methods require more land than conventional farms to achieve the same crop yields, which could be an issue in

---

THE WORLD'S SOIL HOLDS UP TO **3** TIMES AS MUCH CARBON AS IS IN THE ATMOSPHERE

---

future, as the planet has to feed more people. It's thought that the current demand for food could almost double by 2050, if populations grow as predicted and we fail to change our food consumption habits.

However, it is estimated that we could feed every person on Earth today if we fixed inefficiencies in our food systems. One idea is vertical farming, which involves crops being grown in stacked layers or shelves; this

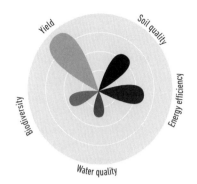

CONVENTIONAL FARMING

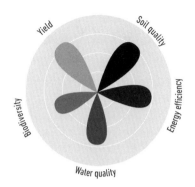

ORGANIC FARMING

▲ While yields are usually lower in organic farming, soil, wildlife, and waterways all fare better, and emissions are reduced.

method would help bring large-scale organic farming into urban centres, reducing transportation emissions and water use, while returning much higher yields of crops and using up to 50% less energy than conventional farming. In addition, moving away from large-scale animal agriculture would free up land to grow crops to feed people directly rather than to feed livestock (see p.34).

Another potential challenge with organic farming is the lack of consistent regulation. In some countries, certain pesticides are permitted to be used on organic crops, causing run-off into waterways, just as in conventional farming.

Despite these reservations, the organic food and farming sectors are growing fast. The EU set a target in 2020 to achieve 25% of agricultural land under organic production by 2030, and other countries have similar ambitions.

Making a switch to organic, where you can, will help support a hugely inventive farming system that balances using the best traditional, low-impact, sustainable techniques with a 21st-century approach to feeding our increasing population.

Buying a bag of organic potatoes might not seem like the most revolutionary act, but every little action supports a community of people forging ways forward to create a greener world. More demand for organic products will lead to a decrease in the amount of land that's industrially farmed, polluted, and stripped of wildlife.

Should I be buying only locally produced food?

This is a difficult question, with a range of different answers that depend on your lifestyle. In general, choosing food that hasn't had too far to travel is a green approach.

The most obvious environmental problem with importing food over long distances is the CO_2 emissions caused by transportation. Ships, lorries, and especially planes all use up fuel and generate emissions and pollution. Refrigerated transport requires even more energy. Often, once air-freighted fruit arrives in its destination country, it is ripened in vast warehouses, which contribute yet more emissions. Complex supply chains also tend to rely heavily on plastic, and having more steps between farm and fork makes it harder to know whether workers at all stages of the chain are treated fairly.

Pros and cons

Avoiding all imported foods isn't necessarily the greenest course of action. There are many cases where

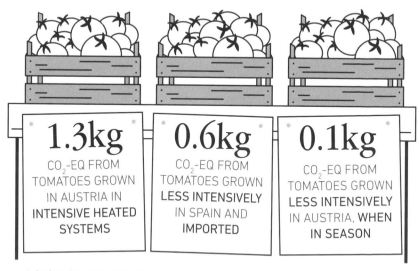

▲ An Austrian study comparing CO_2-equivalent emissions per kilogram of loose tomatoes showed that locally grown can be greener if low-energy farming methods are used.

domestically produced foods have more of an impact than overseas alternatives. Changing your shopping habits might even cause more emissions: a recent thinktank study found that driving to multiple farm shops or independent stores could cost more in emissions than bulk-shipping items to Europe from Africa, for instance. Keeping domestic produce in cold storage for months on end before shipping it around the country also creates more emissions than large-scale freighting.

However, even if buying local produce may not reduce emissions as much as we'd like, it does combat other issues. By sourcing food from local producers you are supporting shorter supply chains – for instance, from farm to you, or from farmer to farm shop to you – which generally means less food waste, less plastic use, and less transportation within the supply chain. You're also investing in the local economy, which supports independent businesses (who generally have a smaller environmental impact than global brands).

Eating seasonally

The best way to ensure that your locally produced fruit or vegetables haven't racked up an unnecessarily large carbon footprint is to eat with the seasons. Seasonal eating has a reduced impact on the planet, as farms aren't forcing fruit and veg to grow at the wrong time of year in energy-heavy artificial conditions: for

example, growing asparagus at Christmas in the UK. Food that is eaten shortly after being harvested, rather than sitting around in refrigerated lorries or on supermarket shelves, is also likely to be more nutritious, as well as tasting fresher.

It's impossible to give clear-cut, simple advice on this issue, because the environmental impact of each food choice you make depends on what the food is, when you're buying it, and where you live. However, a lot of the best advice on the subject comes down to long-held common sense:

- **Choose domestically** produced or local brands when you can – for yogurt, wine, honey, ice cream, chocolate, gin, beer, and more.
- **Local fruit and veg** delivery boxes are brilliant time-saving options if you want to eat more locally and seasonally. A recent study found that they could save CO_2 emissions as well, compared with driving to a farm shop.
- **Learn what ingredients** are grown where you live, and when they are in season (there are charts and lists online), and be guided by this when you shop.
- **Grow your own** vegetables, herbs, or fruit, either in your garden, on an allotment, or in a community garden. This is the best solution for the most local food, and you can help share local food with others. You could also consider keeping your own chickens, if you have space.

How can I find out about the provenance of my food?

Finding out where and how your food was grown is the only way to know how green – or not – it is, and whether your favourite brands are investing in our future.

In a world of mass production and multiple steps between farm and plate, we often have little idea of the journey our food has been on to reach us. Information – often conflicting – is widely available regarding farming practices and the carbon footprints of various foods, but it can be challenging to apply this to the specific items on your shopping list.

The good news is that modern technology is making it easier to track a product's provenance. Blockchain technology (a system of encrypted digital record-keeping, used in a range of industries), is

---

A UK STUDY FOUND THAT

84% OF SHOPPERS CHECK WHERE

THEIR **FOOD HAS COME FROM**

---

making supply chains (see pp.118–119) more transparent. There are now even some apps that will tell you the farm, animal, or field where your food was produced, and the journey it has taken to get to you.

While locally produced food is often the greenest option, it's not always possible to meet all your needs locally. For those items that simply aren't made where you live, look for brands that demonstrate how they support food producers in the country where the product was made. From female-owned farming cooperatives to sustainability-accredited factories powered by renewable energy, the most innovative and forward-thinking food and drinks brands want to shout about and share their ethical credentials.

- **Do your research** – perhaps your preferred supermarket chain has a clearly described policy about sourcing, or your favourite milk alternative, biscuit, or chocolate brand explains the origins of the product on their website.
- **If you're not sure**, then ask. Email the supermarket, local shop, or brand directly and ask them for information on the provenance of a favourite product. If this isn't clear or transparent, then perhaps it's time to find an alternative.

What do all those food certifications mean?

Labels and logos can be confusing when you're trying to do the greenest thing. Beware of greenwashing – some brands aren't as eco as they pretend to be.

It's all too easy for food-producing companies to give the impression of being eco-conscious without the official credentials to back it up. The certifications below are the key ones to look out for when buying food. Not all of these have standardized global symbols, so read labels carefully.

- **Free range** isn't necessarily the assurance you think it is. It merely means the animal has had access to outside space, but doesn't determine for how long or how much space. There is little regulation within this definition, and it varies between countries.
- **Organic** foods, in general, have been grown or reared without the use of chemicals, pesticides, or antibiotics, in a way that is sustainable for the land. However, organic standards vary from country to country, so the specifics will depend on where the food was produced. See pp.46–47 for more details.
- **Fairtrade** means that the product has been farmed or produced fairly, and that everyone in the supply chain is living and working above the poverty line in a workplace free from human-rights abuses.

- **Fairwild** is a global certification that applies to wild plants such as herbs and spices. It promotes sustainable practices throughout the supply chains of these

---

IN 2020 THERE WERE
457 DIFFERENT ECO CERTIFICATIONS
IN USE WORLDWIDE

---

ingredients, and ensures that the people who grow and harvest them are fairly treated and paid.
- **B Corp** is a certification applied to companies rather than products. It is the most difficult sustainability certification to achieve, making it trustworthy across every sector. Certified companies range from tiny independents to global mega-corporations, but all are putting planet and people on a par with profit.

Is it okay to buy plastic-wrapped fruit and veg?

Much as we want to avoid single-use plastic, sometimes it is unavoidable. The occasional plastic wrapper could work out greener overall, by reducing food waste.

As our awareness of plastic pollution has grown, the kneejerk reaction has become to say a clear "no" to all plastic packaging. In many cases, plastic is absolutely unnecessary: if you see apples encased in plastic tubes or shrink-wrapped cabbages, for instance, avoid them. However, many in the food industry argue that plastic wrapping on some items, such as cucumbers and peppers, prolongs shelf life and reduces food waste.

While various alternatives to plastic are being trialled, including algae-based materials or biodegradable wrapping, they aren't widely available yet. But the more you can move away from plastic, the more pressure you put on supermarkets to research, invest in, and adopt non-plastic solutions.

- **Think about shelf life**. Plastic wrapping can be worth it if it means the food won't go off before you manage to eat it – so it's an option for items that are easily damaged, especially if they've already had a long journey to reach the shelves.
- **Support local greengrocers**, farm shops, or zero-waste shops, as they're more likely to sell fruit and veg without plastic packaging.
- **Can you grow your own?** Herbs such as basil and rosemary, for example, come in plastic in the supermarket but are easy to grow in pots on a windowsill or in the garden.

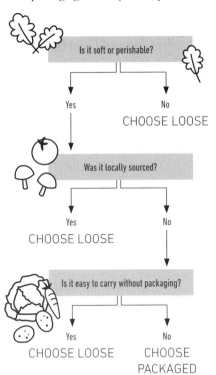

Is it soft or perishable?

Yes → CHOOSE LOOSE (No)

Was it locally sourced?

Yes → CHOOSE LOOSE   No

Is it easy to carry without packaging?

Yes → CHOOSE LOOSE   No → CHOOSE PACKAGED

▲ If you are faced with a choice between packaged and loose versions of the same item, this flowchart may help.

How can I keep food fresh without harming the planet?

Trying to keep your single-use plastic habit down can feel onerous, but adopting a few old-fashioned kitchen hacks really can make a difference.

Clingfilm is one of the easiest and most popular tools for keeping food fresh, but it poses a number of environmental issues. The stretchy plastic is practically impossible to recycle, as it often clogs the machines at recycling facilities. This means that virtually all the clingfilm we use ends up in landfill, incinerators, or the oceans. Once it breaks down into microplastics it becomes even more polluting (see p.96), releasing toxic chemicals and posing a risk to wildlife, especially marine organisms, in whose bodies they accumulate.

Thankfully, there are plenty of ways to protect food and avoid waste without reaching for the clingfilm:

- **Beeswax or soy wax wraps** are a fantastic way to keep food fresh, whether it's your lunchtime sandwich or a bowl of leftovers in the fridge. They are made of pieces of fabric coated in wax, which responds to the heat from your hands by softening and forming a seal. The wraps come in a range of sizes and are reusable – you simply wash them with cold water and washing-up liquid between uses. You can even make them yourself, using bits of surplus fabric and wax, which is available to buy in pellet form. Refresh them by "resetting" the wax in an oven or using an iron.
- **Aluminium foil** can be a suitable alternative to clingfilm. However, the specifics of whether and where it can be recycled vary

---

THE UK USES **ENOUGH CLINGFILM** YEARLY TO WRAP **30** TIMES AROUND THE EQUATOR

---

in different localities. Avoid it if you know you won't be able to recycle it.
- **Avoid plastic** sandwich bags and brand-new plastic food containers, too. Reuse old plastic bags, such as those that arrived as packaging for fruit, veg, or loaves of bread, and old containers such as ice-cream tubs to store food, rather than fuelling the demand for new plastic.

"Our food habits harm biodiversity: 75% of what we eat comes from *just 12 plant species and 5 animal species.*"

Are there foods that just aren't worth the carbon footprint?

While many of the foods on your plate can be produced in more eco-friendly ways, there are some that can't be sustainably produced at the high volumes developed countries demand.

As much as we want a varied diet and are attracted to nutritious superfoods, there is often a price to pay. The sudden adoption of a single ingredient by huge numbers of people can cause that food's carbon footprint to become unjustifiable. Problem foods include:

- **Avocados** – the prime example of this issue. Their rise in popularity, fuelled by health research and Instagram, has encouraged Mexican farmers to destroy ancient forests to expand their avocado farms to meet demand. Add that to the resources and energy needed to pick the fruit, keep them fresh, and transport them across the world, and the result is a carbon-emissions nightmare. There are also ethical issues in many areas, such as parts of Chile, where villagers and smaller farms are denied access to water by larger, corporate-backed plantations.

- **Chia seeds, quinoa**, and coconuts have all had a similar effect: the boom in quinoa, for instance, has led to deforestation and an increase in pesticide use, as Peruvian farmers up production.

- **Bagged salad**, grown under LED lights and transported over long distances, is another carbon-heavy culprit – and who ever finishes a bag, really?

- **King prawns** are mostly farmed in Asia, where their production and harvest damages ancient mangrove swamps, which are essential for the prevention of soil erosion and protection against rising sea levels.

IT CAN TAKE UP TO
320 **LITRES** OF
WATER TO
GROW **ONE AVOCADO**

To ensure your fad foods aren't eco-disasters, research where and how ingredients are produced, and make sure the brands you buy operate a fair-trade or ethically sourced supply chain.

What's the environmental impact of processed foods?

A Western diet, heavy in processed food and snacks, puts more pressure not only on our own health but also on that of our planet.

The biggest environmental issue associated with processed foods is the mass production of the ingredients most commonly used in them, including wheat and maize. These are grown industrially as monocrops, damaging biodiversity and contributing greatly to agricultural pollution. Whereas small-scale, organic, and sustainable farming works with nature to ensure the soil remains healthy, industrial farming does the opposite. It pushes land and livestock as hard as possible for short-term profit at the expense of the environment.

THE **AVERAGE PERSON** IN THE UK RECEIVES **56%** OF THEIR DAILY CALORIE INTAKE FROM **ULTRA-PROCESSED FOODS**

Soil health might not sound exciting, but it is fundamental to a habitable world. In many places, soil is poor in quality: depleted by overuse and spoiled by having been soaked in chemicals. Large-scale farming has decimated everything from the

essential invertebrates and microbes in healthy soil to our ancient forests and wildlife ecosystems. The chemical run-off from fields has created "dead zones" in our oceans, where a lack of oxygen means nothing can live.

Another major problem is the tendency for processed foods to have long supply chains, resulting in food waste and plastic over-use, which have been identified as industry-wide issues. The United Nations has found that farms, manufacturers, and consumer-facing businesses are responsible for 58% of all food waste (see pp.118–19 for more on supply chains and why they are key to solving these issues).

All of that is quite overwhelming when you just want a packet of crisps. But you can make your diet greener:

- **Avoid "ultra-processed"** foods, such as unhealthy snacks, sugary breakfast cereals, and ready-meals.
- **Buy "raw", "whole"**, or organic ingredients when possible.
- **Embrace cooking** from scratch; the satisfaction makes the extra work worthwhile. You'll be helping to reduce food waste (who wastes home-made cake?), cutting back on plastic packaging, and not giving your money to the processed-foods business.

Which is the greenest form of sugar?

Concerned about the consequences of your sweet tooth? While sugar in any form isn't particularly green, some types are more eco-friendly than others.

If a food contains added sugar, it is likely to have come from one of three crops: maize, sugar cane, or sugar beet. High-fructose corn syrup (HFCS), made from maize, is often used in fizzy drinks and convenience foods, for instance; corn sugar, dextrose, and maltodextrin are all also common maize-derived sugars.

Maize is a significant monocrop: it accounts for one-third of all cropland in the US, taking up 36 million hectares of land. The many pesticides needed at this industrial scale of farming damage soil, pollute water, and destroy ecosystems. Maize production uses more fossil fuels and releases more greenhouse gases than the production of sugar cane or beet, and the huge corporations behind HFCS are rarely transparent or ethical in their practices.

Sugar cane and sugar beet, while both farmed in a less damaging way overall than maize, are nonetheless often grown relatively intensively. And, aside from farming, there's the issue of the energy- and water-intensive refining process. Producing enough sugar to satisfy the world's demand can realistically only be done using unsustainable methods; to control the problem, we need to reduce the amount of added sugar we consume.

- **If you do buy** refined sugar, make sure it's Fairtrade or organic, to lessen the environmental impact.
- **Avoid highly processed** foods and fizzy drinks in favour of small-batch, locally produced, or home-made versions – better for you as well as for the planet.

1KG OF SUGAR FROM **SUGAR CANE** HAS A WATER FOOTPRINT OF

1,500 litres

1KG OF SUGAR FROM **SUGAR BEET** HAS A WATER FOOTPRINT OF

935 litres

What's the most eco-friendly way to make a cup of coffee?

From cafetières to slow-drip filter machines, there have never been more ways to make coffee – but not every cup has the same carbon footprint.

Much of the environmental impact of making coffee comes from growing the beans. The ever-rising global demand for coffee has meant that the traditional method of growing coffee trees in the shade beneath a canopy of taller forest trees has been widely abandoned in favour of large, exposed plantations – a practice that encourages deforestation and requires widespread use of chemical fertilizers. Increasing awareness of the issue is helping to support shade-grown coffee as an ethical consumer choice.

Assessing the greenest way to make a cup of coffee at home means thinking about energy consumption and the amount of coffee needed.

Instant coffee granules and cafetière coffee fare fairly well on both criteria. Instant granules use relatively little coffee per cup. Cafetières have no single-use parts and require only ground coffee and water, so score highly on the eco-stakes. Coffee-pod machines do well in some respects: they need just a small amount of coffee per cup, and their energy consumption is low. However, they do generate a large amount of plastic waste, which

- ☑ BUY ETHICAL COFFEE
- ☑ ONLY MAKE WHAT YOU NEED
- ☑ REUSE THE GROUNDS

has become an issue as the machines have increased in popularity (up to 40% of US households own one).

Some methods are less efficient. Espresso machines, whether stove-top or electric, don't create plastic waste but do use large amounts of coffee and energy to make just one small cup. Drip-filter coffee machines are often on for long periods of time, using up a lot of energy, and most also require single-use filters.

For the most eco-friendly cup of coffee, here's what to do:

- **Use simpler, low-tech** methods to brew coffee, such as a cafetière, rather than electric machines, which take more energy to produce, use, repair, and dispose of.
- **If you have** a pod machine, seek out recyclable aluminium pods or

---

39,000 PLASTIC COFFEE PODS
ARE PRODUCED **EACH MINUTE**

---

biodegradable capsules, and dispose of them appropriately.

- **If you have** a drip-filter machine, use reusable or compostable filters.
- **Choose coffee** with a certification such as Fairtrade or Rainforest Alliance, and, ideally, opt for organic and shade-grown.
- **Reduce waste** by composting your used coffee grounds or sprinkling them directly on soil as a fertilizer and slug-deterrent.

Can I avoid plastic in teabags?

A soothing cup of tea can be a surprising contributor to the plastic problem.

Many teabags contain a pliable plastic called polypropylene, used as a seal. When we make and drink tea, billions of plastic particles leach out into our drinks and then into our bodies. The presence of plastic also means that used teabags don't fully decompose; instead, they contaminate our soil and food waste.

Some tea brands are now making bags entirely from plant materials, but even then, there can be eco issues (for instance, some use corn starch – see p.57 for the environmental issues associated with corn). And while many companies have proudly switched to "biodegradable" bags, in practice the bags will only break down in the hotter temperatures of commercial composters (of which there aren't many in the UK), and not at home.

- **The best solution** is to switch to loose-leaf tea, choosing ethically traded, organic options, ideally from a zero-waste store. Brew your leaves in a teapot or use a reusable filter.
- **If you use teabags**, choose a brand that uses organic, sustainably produced ingredients, and no plastic.

Are reusable coffee cups really greener than takeaway cups?

Grabbing a coffee on the go may be convenient, but it creates waste and adds to global carbon emissions. Tweaking your cafe habit can reduce your coffee's eco-impact.

Single-use coffee cups are a visible sign of our convenience-driven lifestyles – 2.8 billion of them are used each year in Germany, for instance. Most are made from plastic-coated paper, and while some companies offer "compostable" or recyclable cups, the reality is that the infrastructure needed for these processes simply isn't in place yet. The vast majority of cups still go to landfill, where there isn't the air, moisture, or bacteria needed to break them down.

Investing in a reusable coffee cup is a step in the right direction, but just how green this solution is depends on how much you use your cup. The materials and energy used to manufacture them mean that even a cup made from polypropylene, one of the lowest-impact options, needs to be used 20 times before it works out greener than a throwaway cup. And some take even longer to offset: polycarbonate cups don't overtake disposables until around their 65th use.

To ensure your daily coffee has less of an eco-impact:

- **Forego coffees** on the move: instead, build in time to enjoy your drink in a café, using a ceramic cup.
- **If you want** a coffee on the go, make it yourself at home and put it in a reusable cup or flask to drink on your morning commute.
- **If you're not** ready to give up your takeaway coffee habit, always carry a reusable cup. Choosing a plastic-free one is a good idea, as long as you use it enough times to offset the environmental cost of its production and disposal.

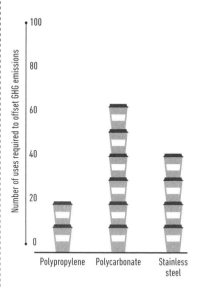

▲ Each type of reusable cup needs to be used many times to keep its lifetime carbon emissions below that of the equivalent number of disposable cups.

What's the greenest way to enjoy soft drinks?

There's no denying that the soft-drinks industry has burdened the planet with a mountain of plastic waste. But eco-friendly solutions for quenching your thirst are out there.

The global soft-drinks industry is responsible for an enormous amount of plastic pollution. For example, an estimated 34 billion single-use plastic bottles end up in the ocean each year. The top three companies responsible for the most plastic pollution all produce soft drinks. Many soft-drinks and bottled-water producers claim that their bottles are both recycled and recyclable; however, although this equates to less oil used to make the plastic in the first place, the energy used in the recycling process still generates huge amounts of emissions.

The other issue with soft drinks is what's in them. Mass-produced drinks are often sweetened with high-fructose corn syrup (HFCS – see p.57), which is produced using unsustainable farming methods. Many also contain ingredients such as vanilla and stevia, which are frequently associated with unethical practices, such as land grabs that are carried out without the consent of indigenous communities.

There is also the issue of water use. It takes up to 170 litres of water to make just 0.5 litres of carbonated drink – in a world where 785 million people don't have access to clean water.

A greener approach to soft drinks means consuming less:

- **Avoid buying** drinks in plastic bottles. When you're out and about, carry a reusable water bottle instead.
- **If you're a fan of fizz**, consider making your own drinks by investing in a home carbonator, where canisters are recycled and bottles reused. Up to 20% of Swedes have already adopted this practice.

A HOME CARBONATOR CAN TAKE

550 SINGLE-USE PLASTIC BOTTLES OUT OF CIRCULATION EACH YEAR

- **If you do buy** soft drinks, choose ones made with natural ingredients and fewer additives and sweeteners, and which are sold in recyclable aluminium cans or glass bottles.

Is wine bad for the planet?

Innovations in wine production over the last hundred years have turned out to be a backwards step environmentally. A shift to greener production methods is something to raise a glass to.

There is a big difference between mass-market wine, produced on vast estates, and wine created by artisans in small vineyards or by cooperatives that employ low-intervention methods, nurturing the land to invest in its future. Many big wine estates farm on an industrial scale using huge amounts of pesticides, which damages soil health and creates chemical run-off into waterways. Combined with the ecological impact of cultivating a single crop over a huge area, this wreaks havoc on local biodiversity.

Seeds of change

The soil degradation that has resulted from heavy pesticide use on these larger estates has forced many

VINEYARDS COVER **3% OF FRANCE'S LAND** BUT USE **20%** OF ITS PESTICIDES

wine-producing countries to adopt greener practices. Almost all wineries in New Zealand have committed to a sustainable certification, and 75% of Chile's vineyards have passed a similar accreditation. And in 2019,

Sonoma County in California became the first wine-growing region to be certified almost entirely sustainable, with 99% of its acerage accredited.

Each country has its own certification, but the main tenets involve avoiding pesticides and other artificial involvement in the wine's production, and promoting natural, permaculture solutions (see p.158). So, what should you look out for when cultivating a more eco-friendly approach to wine buying?

- **Choose wine labelled** "low intervention", "biodynamic", "natural", or "organic" (though few wines claim to be organic, as this is a very strict standard to achieve).
- **Look beyond the label** of your favourite wine and research where the grape came from. If you live near a vineyard, buy local to reduce the air miles on your bottle.
- **Don't dismiss** boxed wine or wine from a keg – both equate to lower transportation emissions than wine in glass bottles. Boxed wine also lasts longer once opened.
- **If you're vegan**, keep in mind that most wine contains animal products. Check the labels for animal-derived sulphites, used in the refining process, or choose "unfiltered" wines.

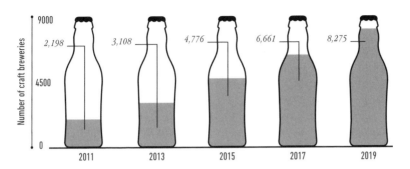

▼ The number of craft breweries in the US has risen quickly over the past decade.

Number of craft breweries

9000

4500

0

2,198 — 2011
3,108 — 2013
4,776 — 2015
6,661 — 2017
8,275 — 2019

Can beer and spirits be eco-friendly?

Drinking beer and spirits sustainably means looking at each brand's production methods and ethos.

Beer- and spirit-making are energy- and water-intensive processes. Brewing beer requires energy for lighting, compressing air, heating, cooling, and refrigeration. On top of this, it takes around 5–6 pints of water to make each pint of beer, and the used grain ends up as solid waste. Bottled beer is also heavy to transport.

Complex distilling methods used to produce spirits also have a high energy demand and result in significant water and pulp wastage (what's left over of the raw materials after the alcohol has been made). The ingredients can be problematic, too: rum, for instance, is made with sugar cane, which has its own environmental impact (see p.57).

Thankfully, thousands of pioneering brands are pursuing ethical practices.

- **Look for locally brewed** craft beers that source ingredients close to home and use innovative techniques to be greener. These include saving water, investing in renewable energy, or even using surplus bread instead of virgin hops, which cuts down on solid waste. Some breweries donate their profits to charity or invest in projects to help local communities.

- **Choose spirits** made by responsible companies that reduce waste and use sustainably grown ingredients; for example, small-batch tequila makers who use every part of the agave plant and compost the waste, or gin distilleries using local botanicals.

Is there an eco-friendly way to barbecue?

Our fondness for barbecues comes at a cost. What you use to light your fire – and the food you cook on it – can make al fresco dining a more or less eco-friendly endeavour.

Both gas and charcoal-lit barbecues release carbon dioxide, but charcoal is the bigger culprit when it comes to pollution – it releases twice the amount of toxic particles into the air as gas, harming our respiratory health and the environment. What's more, the mass-produced charcoal bricks that many of us use are made from unsustainably logged tropical wood and coated in chemicals to make them easier to ignite. Disposable charcoal barbecues are the most harmful of all. As well as being energy-inefficient, they are covered in single-use plastic and are non-recyclable.

While gas has less of an impact on air quality than charcoal, it is still a non-renewable fossil fuel, so

---

THE UK USES MORE THAN
1,000,000
DISPOSABLE BARBECUES
EVERY YEAR

---

isn't the greenest choice. Electric barbecue grills can be a better option, provided your electricity comes from a renewable source (see p.134).

If you're planning to cook al fresco, here's what to keep in mind:

- **For both gas** and charcoal barbecues, use a lid so you can control the temperature and thereby use less fuel.
- **If you buy charcoal**, try to source bricks from sustainably managed native woodland. Though a bit pricier, their structure means they typically burn for longer than mass-produced varieties, so fewer bricks are needed.
- **Choose natural firelighters**, made from materials such as wood shavings, over mainstream, petroleum-based versions.
- **If you're using a firepit**, burn logs made from materials such as coffee-bean waste or recycled sawdust, which produce less smoke than wood.
- **When choosing barbecue** food, cut back on meat and fish and choose vegetarian or vegan options. Grilled vegetables such as mushrooms, artichokes, and aubergines are truly delicious. Make your own salads rather than buying pre-packed ones, and get out the china plates and glasses rather than using throwaway versions.

How can I be green when having a picnic?

With all those single-serving, plastic-packaged snacks and drinks, picnics often mean waste. But a little planning goes a long way in helping the planet.

The often-spontaneous nature of picnics can mean that green concerns go out of the window. The temptation is to overbuy and opt for convenience over sustainability, resulting in a haul of plastic-packaged foods such as punnets of strawberries, quiche in foil trays, and small pots of dips and spreads, together with throwaway cups and plastic cutlery. Even home-prepared food is usually wrapped in clingfilm, destined for landfill, or in aluminium foil, much of which we then fail to recycle.

There is also the issue of food waste, with fresh food that has been sitting out in warm conditions being much more likely to end up in the bin than taken home and eaten later.

- **For the greenest picnics**, plan ahead. Make sandwiches, salads, cakes, and other food at home. Invest in a range of reusable containers, bags, and wraps. Try beeswax or soy wax wraps (see p.53) instead of clingfilm to keep food sealed and fresh.
- **If you don't have time** to make food, take containers from home to fill straight from the deli counter – many supermarkets are happy to do this now. Bring reusable cutlery and washable napkins (see p.31), too.

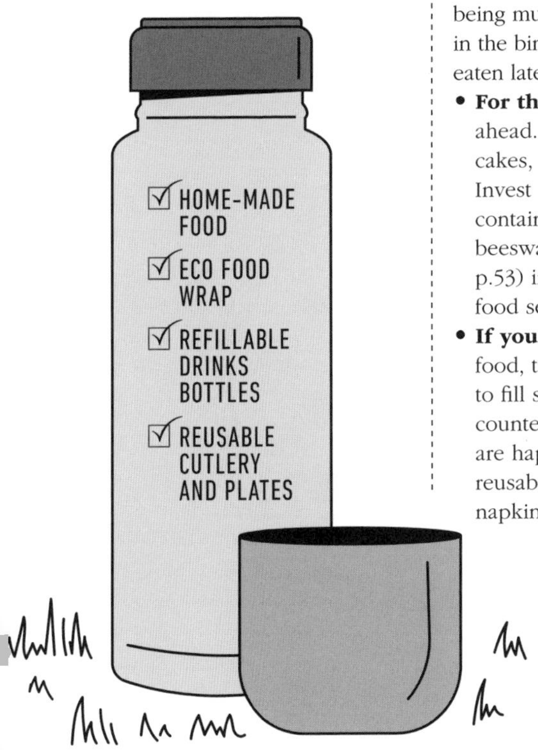

☑ HOME-MADE FOOD

☑ ECO FOOD WRAP

☑ REFILLABLE DRINKS BOTTLES

☑ REUSABLE CUTLERY AND PLATES

◀ If you picnic often, invest in zero-waste picnic essentials.

How can I dine out ethically?

Eating out doesn't have to mean leaving your green intentions at the door. Choosing a restaurant carefully can help you apply the same eco standards you have at home.

The restaurant industry is a major contributor to the issue of global food waste. In the UK, the sector clocks up nearly 200,000 tonnes of food waste annually. It's estimated that one-third of that is simply food left uneaten on customers' plates.

Restaurants also have a detrimental impact on air quality in urban areas. Particle pollution from the cooking process has been found to be denser near areas with a higher number of eating establishments. In London, for example, commercial cooking is estimated to account for 13% of this type of air pollution.

Greener choices

While factors such as cooking processes may be beyond your control, you can research a restaurant's policy on waste, and whether it uses local suppliers to shorten the supply chain and eliminate air miles. In terms of waste alone, it's not always the

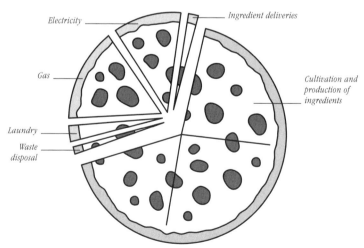

Electricity

Ingredient deliveries

Gas

Cultivation and production of ingredients

Laundry

Waste disposal

▲ This breakdown of the carbon footprint of a typical restaurant in New York shows that ingredients are by far the biggest factor.

case that chain restaurants are the worst offenders while independents are blemish-free. One well-established UK high-street chain is known for donating all its surplus food to charities.

If you are discerning when eating out, ensuring that your consumer power supports restaurants that are striving for sustainability, it becomes harder for less eco-friendly establishments to carry on ignoring the issues we're facing. By choosing thoughtfully, you can have a say in the ingredients that your favourite restaurants use – and since ingredients are responsible for the largest portion of a restaurant's carbon footprint, making them greener is an effective way to shrink that footprint. Bear in mind the following:

- **Think about** locality and seasonality. When looking at a menu, be mindful of air miles and field-to-fork traceability. Go for whatever is in season and, if possible, locally produced. Favour restaurants that are transparent about the provenance of their food and commit to using ingredients that haven't racked up a hefty carbon footprint.
- **Avoid industrially** farmed meat. Livestock production accounts for 15% of all greenhouse-gas emissions. If you don't want to give up eating meat when dining out, choose restaurants that use locally reared, pasture-fed, organic meat. If an establishment isn't clear about the provenance

of its meat, speak to the staff about it, to raise awareness of the issue.
- **Don't order** "at-risk" fish. Make sure you are clued up on which fish are currently sustainable where you live (see p.39).

A SURVEY FOUND THAT
66% OF RESPONDENTS WERE WILLING TO SPEND MORE **TO DINE OUT SUSTAINABLY**

- **Think about waste**. Avoid all-you-can-eat buffets – some of the worse offenders – and order only what you think you'll manage to eat. If you're sharing plates, order smaller amounts and add more later, rather than over-ordering from the start. Seek out restaurants that proudly use as much of a product as possible, whether "nose to tail" of a meat product, or "root to fruit" of plant-based ingredients. And don't be shy about asking for a doggy bag – or take along your own container – to stop the food you've paid for going to waste.
- **Support the** restaurant workers, for instance by checking that your tip goes to the waiters, chef, and washing-up staff, rather than lining a corporation's or owner's pockets.

Should I avoid eating fast food?

Many of us love the taste and convenience of fast food and takeaways, but cheap burgers and fried chicken embody serious eco-issues. It's time to slow down.

Fast food is a 570-billion-dollar industry that relies on industrial-scale agriculture to keep prices attractive to people wanting a quick, convenient meal. The scale of the global fast-food market is truly mind-boggling: one burger chain sells 75 burgers a second; another fast-food brand gets through one billion chickens a year. This demand for ingredients is met by large-scale factory farming, which generates a huge quantity of greenhouse-gas

IT'S ESTIMATED THAT

40% OF ALL LITTER IS

FAST-FOOD PACKAGING

emissions, as well as driving deforestation and polluting the water and land around the farms. It also commandeers a vast amount of land and water in order to feed and rear the animals that are used to make your milkshakes and chicken nuggets (see p.34 for more on why industrial meat production is terrible for the planet).

Then there are the styrofoam containers and greasy pizza boxes, which can't be recycled, as well as endless plastic bags, disposable sets of cutlery, sauce sachets, and plastic cups. These things all take energy and resources to manufacture and transport, but quickly end up either burnt or sent to landfill. The US alone goes through two billion cardboard pizza boxes a year.

While many fast-food chains have adopted targets to reduce their water and energy usage and cut down on how much their dairy and meat production impacts our planet, there is a long way to go. Here's what you can do to be greener:

- **Avoid fast food** where possible. If you want to make a meaningful change to your eating habits to help the planet, but aren't ready to adopt a vegan or vegetarian lifestyle, giving up takeaways and fast food is a great first step.
- **If you need** something quick and convenient, aim to choose vegan or vegetarian options, ideally in packaging that is recyclable and as minimal as possible.
- **Choose local**, independent restaurants who share where their ingredients come from, rather than global chains.
- **Say no to** plastic bags and disposable cutlery, and reuse plastic takeaway containers (as well as any leftovers).

10% OF ALL **FOOD** SERVED AT WEDDINGS **GOES TO WASTE**

How can I be green when catering for large numbers?

Whatever the occasion, feeding a large group while trying to stay eco-friendly can seem daunting, but it's possible.

A special event such as a party or wedding can generate a lot of waste, from any food that doesn't get eaten and items such as disposable plates, plastic cutlery, and napkins.

There's no reason why these issues can't be avoided, though: in some ways, feeding large numbers is an ideal opportunity to be greener without much extra effort. Buying and cooking in bulk means less packaging, more, efficient, one-pot cooking, and less washing-up than when you're cooking for smaller numbers, which all helps to reduce your carbon footprint.

There are plenty of ways to cut down the eco-impact and still enjoy sharing a feast:

- **Plan carefully** to avoid ending up with more food than you'll need.
- **Stick to a plant-based** menu and, if needed, provide meat or cheese as an add-on. Curries, traybakes, and dhals lend themselves to being vegan, and stretch humble ingredients to feed lots of people.
- **Use reusable crockery** and cutlery – borrowed or rented if necessary. Or, if you need everything to be disposable, use cardboard plates and sustainably sourced bamboo cutlery, and make sure they get recycled.
- **Ask guests to** bring along food containers so that any leftovers can be taken home and eaten.

GREEN
BATHROOM

Which is greener, a bath or shower?

This sounds like a simple one, but how efficient your shower is depends on how you're using it. Speeding up your routine a little could save a lot of water.

While it might seem like a bath uses up a lot more water than a shower, that's not necessarily the case. The average tub holds 136 litres, while the average shower pumps out 19 litres of water per minute (unless you install a water-saving shower head).

7 minutes (less water than a bath)

9 minutes (average shower time)

▲ If your shower lasts longer than 7 minutes, it's no better water-wise than a bath, so cut down shower time if you can.

That means showering for more than 7 minutes uses at least the amount of water in a full bath.

According to a UK environmental charity, the average length of time we spend in the shower is 9 minutes, with 7% of people running it for a full 3 minutes while they do other tasks before getting in.

A shower is only the greenest option if it doesn't go on for too long. Reducing your water usage can be easy, with some simple changes to your usual habits:

- **If you shower**, use a timer to limit the time you're in there (a good rule of thumb is to shower for as long as your favourite song – around 3–4 minutes).
- **Fit a water-saving** shower head if you can. These reduce the amount of water used by up to 26 litres for a 7-minute shower; they might not be very efficient if you have low water pressure, but otherwise, think of the savings!
- **If you have a bath**, don't fill it too high; and once you're done, reuse the water to water plants.
- **Fit a water meter** so you can see how much water you're actually using, and set yourself goals to cut back. You'll save money, too.

What's the greenest way to shave?

Whether you're shaving your shins or your sideburns, your razor shouldn't be considered as disposable as your unwanted hair. Long-lasting reusable razors eliminate plastic waste.

Billions of disposable razors end up in landfill each year. While the steel blades can be recycled, most aren't, and the plastic handles do nothing but pile up. Adding to the plastic problem, many are sold in thick plastic packaging. Remarkably, very few recycling programmes exist for disposable razors.

You could look for razors with handles made of sustainable, fast-growing bamboo or recycled plastic, both of which help cut down plastic waste. Even better, though, is returning to a longer-lasting product that you invest in for life.

Electric shavers avoid the need for water and the energy to heat it; they also last for several years. On the other hand, they are environmentally costly to produce in the first place, require batteries (see p.140), and can't be recycled. All these things, along with the electricity they use, mean that over their lifetime electric razors are only marginally better for the planet than disposable razors.

The greenest option by far is an old-fashioned safety razor, which is made of steel and can be fitted with replaceable double-edged blades. Shaving with one requires a bit more care and patience than

THE AVERAGE **DISPOSABLE RAZOR** IS USED ONLY

6–9 TIMES BEFORE BEING **BINNED**

with disposables, but it's worth it to avoid the plastic waste. Online companies have popped up offering on-demand delivery services for safety razors (which shortens the supply chain – see p.118), often combined with traditional, plastic-free shaving soap, and packaged in cardboard.

Foams and lotions

Another way to make your grooming routine greener is to stop using shaving foam. Aside from containing harmful chemicals, which affect our water and marine life, aerosol cans cannot be recycled, and take 500 years to break down. Switch to lotions, creams, or soaps in plastic-free packaging, making sure the ones you use don't contain palm oil or a harmful alternative (see p.44).

If waxing is more your style, choose a natural sugar wax that's free from plastic and synthetic chemicals.

Should I use bars of soap and shampoo or refillable bottles?

Bottled soap, shower gel, and shampoo may be convenient, but they're big contributors to pollution. The good news is that there are plenty of options that avoid plastic and synthetic chemicals.

Liquid soaps, scrubs, and hair products contribute vast amounts of plastic to landfills. The US alone produces over half a billion shampoo bottles a year – and that doesn't include hotel miniatures. In the UK, only 50% of people say they recycle their bathroom plastic; in the US it's around 20%. The plastic pump bottles that liquid hand soap comes in are often made from single-use plastic that can't be recycled (the pumps make it almost impossible).

Even if you're able to refill your bottles, liquid soaps and shampoos aren't great for the planet. Compared with solid versions, they require more water and energy to produce, are less efficient to transport, and contain synthetic chemicals that, once in waterways, can harm wildlife.

Joining the solid-soap party? Look for small-batch (which avoid wasted ingredients) or handmade bars. Many come wrapped in paper, cardboard, or no packaging at all. Using bars

▼ Solid soap and shampoo bars require less energy, packaging, and transport than liquid versions, as well as lasting longer.

LIQUID SOAP USES **5 X** MORE ENERGY TO PRODUCE, **20 X** MORE PACKAGING, AND **15 X** MORE TRANSPORT EMISSIONS THAN SOLID SOAP

SOLID SOAP LASTS **7 X** AS LONG AS THE SAME WEIGHT OF LIQUID SOAP

made in your local area will reduce your morning routine's air miles. Choose all-natural ingredients – there are plenty of vegan versions too, made with vegetable glycerine, olive oil, or shea butter instead of tallow and other animal fats.

Solid options are also greener when it comes to shower gel and body scrubs, as well as shampoo and conditioner. Washing your hair without using mainstream shampoo no longer means resorting to vinegar rinses or putting up with weeks of grease to achieve a self-cleansing

---

THE **CARBON FOOTPRINT** OF LIQUID HAND SOAP IS

25% **LARGER** THAN THAT OF SOAP BARS

---

curtain of glossy hair (though there's no harm in trying either of these zero-waste options). Solid bars last two or three times longer than liquid shampoo. They tend to be free of sodium lauryl sulphate (SLS), which is what makes shampoos lather, so you might not get as many suds, but this isn't what cleans your hair, so don't panic. Different bars will suit different hair types, so experiment – it might take your hair a few washes to get used to a new formula. They are great for air travel too: invest in a travel case and wave goodbye to 100ml-bottle restrictions.

How can I make sure my deodorant is eco-friendly?

Choosing green products and smelling good is easy when you know what to look for.

No one wants to pong, but you don't want to pollute either. Mainstream deodorants come in either aerosols or plastic roll-ons, both of which aren't generally recyclable. Many of them also contain potentially harmful ingredients such as parabens, which are preservatives, and aluminium, which prevents sweat by clogging pores; some studies suggest these can cause cancers and other health issues.

Natural deodorants don't contain aluminium, but they do vary in their ingredients much more than regular ones, and suit different skin types. So finding your perfect product might take a bit of trial and error.

- **Look for plastic-free**, solid, all-natural deodorants in metal tins and cardboard tubes, or creams in glass jars. If you're struggling to find them in high-street stores, look online.
- **If you prefer,** you can make your own using various combinations of shea butter, coconut oil, arrowroot, baking soda, and essential oils; search online for recipes.

What's the environmental impact of toilet paper?

While much of the world cleans with water rather than paper in the bathroom, the impact of toilet paper on the planet is still enormous – and it's not just about the trees.

Not to put a downer on your alone time, but toilet paper is a huge drain on the planet's resources. A growing demand for luxury brands has led to a decline in the production of recycled toilet roll. The result is that the majority of toilet roll today is made from virgin wood pulp, often from unsustainable sources. The pulp is formed via an energy-intensive process and then bleached using complex chemicals, which release carcinogens such as dioxins into the atmosphere. Furthermore, a recent report calculated that manufacturing just one roll of toilet paper requires 168 litres of water. Now think about that at scale – the average person in the developed world gets through two rolls a week.

It might sound counterintuitive, but bidets and water jets are less wasteful of water compared to toilet roll. According to one estimate, the average bidet uses less than half a litre of water per use, which is much, much less than the amount consumed to make toilet paper. So bidets are the greener option, saving both water and trees. The popularity, and availability, of bidets varies greatly from country to country, but those that have embraced them – such

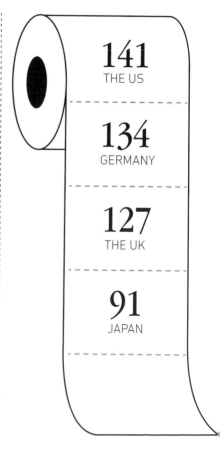

141
THE US

134
GERMANY

127
THE UK

91
JAPAN

▲ In a 2018 study estimating the number of rolls of toilet paper used annually per capita, these countries were the top four.

as Venezuela, where 90% of homes have one – might be on the right track.

- **Consider installing** a jet wash attachment to your toilet seat, or, if plumbing allows, a bidet.
- **As a greener alternative** to toilet roll, use cut-up, upcycled reusable cloths to wipe; they can be placed in a bag or receptacle after use, ready to be put through the washing machine.
- **If you want** to stick to toilet paper, switch to recycled options. Look for brands that deliver boxes of 100% recycled rolls without plastic packaging. You can also try toilet paper made of FSC-certified bamboo, rather than wood pulp. Virgin wood pulp is made from slow-growing deciduous trees as well as faster-growing coniferous ones (see p.169 for more on the FSC). Be aware of the "FSC Mix" logo, which means the roll contains virgin wood pulp, and, above all, avoid "luxury" toilet roll or 4-ply, which use far more virgin pulp per roll than basic brands. Is it worth the extra comfort if you're contributing to the destruction of forests every time you wipe?

How much water does it take to flush the loo?

Water scarcity is a growing issue. By making some simple changes you can stop your toilet wasting water.

Flushing the toilet accounts for around 30% of the use of fresh water in European homes. Dual-flush toilets – which give the option of a shorter flush for liquid waste only – use up to 6 litres per flush, but older toilets without this function can use up to 13 litres. Most people flush a toilet five times a day on average, using as much as 65 litres.

There are a few things you can do to limit how much water you flush away each day:

- **Place a water-filled** plastic bottle, inflatable bag, or brick into your cistern, to reduce the amount of water per flush.
- **Reduce** the number of times you flush. Do you have to flush each time you pass urine, for instance during the night?
- **Check for leaks** in your toilet – a leaky cistern will waste water (and money), so needs investigating.
- **If you're buying** a new toilet, choose a dual-flush model if available (and use it properly).

Is there a greener way to manage my periods?

For many of us, disposable sanitary products are so much the norm that reusable options seem unthinkable. But the time has come to face up to the huge environmental cost of periods.

Sanitary products play a big role in polluting the planet – all those pads and tampons thrown away every month contain significant amounts of plastic and will take up to 500 years to break down. The average woman in the developed world will get through 11,000 tampons or pads during her reproductive years. In the UK alone, 2.5 million tampons – and often, their plastic applicators too – are flushed down the toilet every day, with many ending up in our rivers and seas, or washed up on shorelines. In 2016, a survey by a UK charity found 20 items of sanitary waste for every 100 metres of coast that was inspected.

Waste isn't the only issue when it comes to the eco-impact of your period. As well as plastics, sanitary products use materials (including wood pulp) that have been bleached, and contain chlorine and dioxins – chemicals that are hazardous to human health, and which, if they leach into the soil, can pollute groundwater and destroy soil fertility. Also, their manfacturing processes are energy-heavy and polluting.

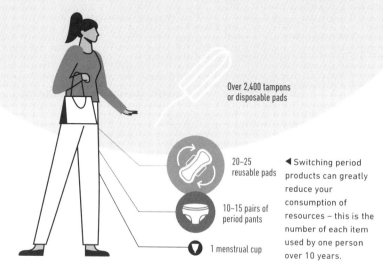

Over 2,400 tampons or disposable pads

20–25 reusable pads

10–15 pairs of period pants

1 menstrual cup

◀ Switching period products can greatly reduce your consumption of resources – this is the number of each item used by one person over 10 years.

So how can we reduce the impact of the modern menstruation industry on our planet?

- **If you do buy** disposable products, swap to brands that use paper wraps and cardboard tubes or reusable applicators. Beware, however, of "plant-based plastic" alternatives – they may claim to biodegrade more quickly, but in reality they often don't. Look for

10 billion
PLASTIC TAMPON APPLICATORS ARE **THROWN AWAY** EVERY MONTH **WORLDWIDE**

sanitary pads made entirely from renewable materials, and tampons made from organic cotton or similarly biodegradable alternatives. You could shorten the supply chain by subscribing to a service that delivers sanitary products to your door monthly. Also, consider buying from companies that donate products or profits to projects tackling period poverty – millions of women worldwide cannot afford, or have no access to, any kind of sanitary protection.

- **Switch to a reusable method**; this can seem daunting to generations brought up on single-use sanitary products, but reusable options are indisputably the best solution to the period

problem. Period pants are a washable, all-in-one, pants/pad combination, made from moisture-wicking cotton and absorbent fabric, with an antimicrobial, leak-resistant lining. Although only millimeters thick, most period pants can hold two tampons' worth of blood. They last for a couple of years and come in a range of styles to suit both heavy and lighter days. Another good option is removable reusable pads. Many have "wings" and poppers so they can be used securely with normal underwear. For a really zero-cost, zero-waste option, you could even make your own pads from fabric scraps – search "reusable sanitary pad patterns" online. Finally, another excellent reusable option that's growing in popularity is the silicone menstrual cup. This is inserted into the vagina like a tampon, where it collects your menstrual flow inside your body, and is then removed and emptied. After a quick wash, it's ready to be inserted again – and it can be sterilized in boiling water between periods. One cup lasts around 10 years, so by helping the planet, you can also save yourself a considerable amount of cash!

How can I choose sustainable and zero-waste skincare products?

Adopting a more sustainable skincare routine means looking at two things: the ingredients your products contain, and the packaging they come in.

Despite being sold on the high street, many skincare products contain ingredients that can harm you and the planet. Parabens and other preservatives can cause hormone imbalances, and other common ingredients, including sodium lauryl sulphate (SLS) and diethanolamine (DEA), have been shown to be carcinogenic. Palm oil (see p.44) is another prevalent skincare ingredient.

The skincare industry also contributes to plastic pollution, with many tubes, tubs, and bottles being difficult to recycle. And it's not just packaging: individually wrapped sheet masks are a single-use plastic nightmare, and microbeads – now banned in many countries – have caused havoc for our marine life.

- **Look for organic** and natural ingredients, such as cocoa butter, avocado, essential oils, and even foraged botanicals. Try exfoliants made with waste coffee grounds or sugar scrubs (or make your own). Keep in mind that not all natural skincare is vegan, as many use

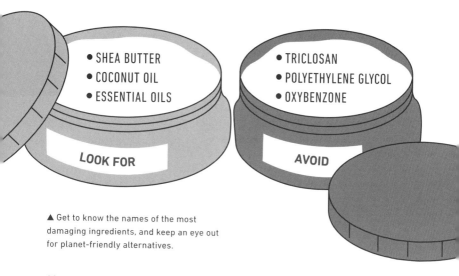

- SHEA BUTTER
- COCONUT OIL
- ESSENTIAL OILS

LOOK FOR

- TRICLOSAN
- POLYETHYLENE GLYCOL
- OXYBENZONE

AVOID

▲ Get to know the names of the most damaging ingredients, and keep an eye out for planet-friendly alternatives.

sustainably sourced beeswax or honey in place of synthetic ingredients, but most independent brands are transparent about what they use. The EU and countries including India, Israel, and New Zealand have banned animal testing of skincare products, but it still goes on in many areas, so check that your favourite brand doesn't participate.

- **Choosing products** made near you is greener than ordering a cult eco-brand from halfway around the world. If you can, buy direct from the brand or at a local market. Support brands that manufacture in small batches, using natural ingredients grown or foraged in the area.

- **Look for the FairWild** global certification, which guarantees best practice in land management and for workers.

- **Buy fewer products** by picking ones that multi-task, such as balms and oils that can be used on the body, face, and hands, or that act as lip balm, salve, and moisturiser.

- **To cut down on packaging**, choose products that come in biodegradable (cardboard) or recyclable (glass) materials, or that need no packaging at all. Support organic, plastic-free skincare brands that use compostable or recyclable packaging, have created return – and refill –schemes, or are designing solid skincare products with no packaging.

How bad is suncream for the ocean?

The importance of wearing suncream can't be overstated, but its skin-protecting properties harm our oceans.

In one year alone, 14,000 tonnes of suncream can end up swirling in the sea, where chemicals such as oxybenzone disrupt micro-organisms, cause hormonal imbalances which travel up the food chain, and damage coral. Palau and Hawaii have both already banned suncreams that include oxybenzone.

There are a few good choices you can make for a more eco-friendly approach:

- **Look for organic** and/or vegan suncreams that don't contain oxybenzone, parabens, petrochemicals, or propylene glycol.

- **Choose suncream** that comes in recyclable packaging, such as a sugar cane or cardboard tube, a metal tin, or recycled plastic.

- **If you do use** mainstream brands, avoid spray versions, as you have less control about where the lotion ends up (often on the sand or grass as well as your skin).

How do I know if my makeup is eco-friendly?

The beauty industry is booming, but its environmental impact isn't a pretty sight. Putting a green face on means cutting down on unsustainable ingredients and excess packaging.

Your makeup bag can be a mixed bag of eco-issues. Palm oil, used in makeup for texture and longevity, appears in 70% of all cosmetics, but unsustainable production of it causes mass deforestation, destroys habitats, and releases greenhouse gases (see p.44). Most makeup also contains chemicals such as parabens and oxybenzone, which pollute the environment and can be harmful to animals and humans. Many cosmetics companies also still test their products on animals. And, to cap it all, the beauty industry creates more than 142 billion units of packaging a year, the vast majority of which is plastic.

On the whole, makeup made with organic, natural ingredients is the way to go. Keep in mind, though, that there is no regulation of the makeup industry on what can be labelled organic, so it's worth doing your own research about what particular brands put in their products.

- **Support smaller**, independent, and local brands: your money will be going to companies that invest in your local economy, rather than a multinational's profits. Independent producers tend to manufacture with fewer emissions, and by buying locally you're also cutting down on air miles.
- **Choose makeup** that is certified by Cruelty Free International (the "leaping bunny" symbol), People for the Ethical Treatment of Animals (PETA), or the Vegan

☑ NO SYNTHETIC CHEMICALS

☑ CRUELTY-FREE

☑ PALM-OIL-FREE

☑ MINIMAL PACKAGING

☑ LOCALLY PRODUCED

☑ NATURAL INGREDIENTS

▲ Think of green makeup's eco-friendly credentials as a checklist – the more you can tick off, the better.

Society. Animal-testing policies are often hidden in the depths of multinational brands' websites, but smaller, independent brands tend to be more open, with higher eco standards.

- **Look for the global** certification Roundtable on Sustainable Palm Oil (RSPO), which ensures a sustainable supply chain and fairly paid farmers.
- **To reduce packaging**, look for makeup that uses a refill system.

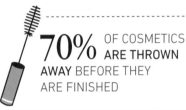

70% OF COSMETICS ARE THROWN AWAY BEFORE THEY ARE FINISHED

This way, you keep the plastic containers and order refills of, for instance, pressed powder or lipstick. There are also brands that package their products in cardboard, bamboo, or recycled materials, and some solid makeup brands need little packaging at all. Switching to more multi-use products is also a great way to reduce single-use plastic, and means you're lugging around less in your makeup bag.

- **Try making your own** makeup – DIY recipes for blusher, lip-stain, and more are flourishing online and make use of natural ingredients and your own containers.

What's the greenest way to remove makeup?

Being more eco-friendly during your end-of-the-day routine means going back to basics.

Every year we're sold new miracle products to keep our makeup on longer or help it come off more easily, but many of them are far from eco-friendly, with makeup wipes being the worst offenders. The world gets through 1.3 billion wet wipes a day, and each one takes 100 years or more to biodegrade. Not only are they an eco-disaster, they aren't even very effective, wiping makeup and bacteria around your face rather than lifting them off.

The greenest makeup removal options are also the simplest, and the most natural. Switch to reusable alternatives, such as organic cotton pads or muslin cloths that can be washed, and are better for your skin.

Instead of buying synthetic cleansers in plastic bottles, try using the plain old cooking oils in your kitchen (coconut or olive oil are best – choose organic and cold-pressed), or look for planet-friendly brands using ingredients such as seaweed extracts, essential oils, witch hazel, and shea butter, in glass jars or refillable bottles.

Are there environmentally friendly ways to dye or relax my hair?

Ammonia, sodium hydroxide, and other chemicals used to transform our tresses can mess with the microorganisms in our water and have consequences for marine life.

Mainstream hair dye includes several damaging chemicals, such as ammonia, which pollutes the air and acidifies water, and paraphenylene-diamine (PPD), a skin irritant and allergen. Relaxants to straighten hair also contain harsh chemicals such as sodium hydroxide. When washed down the drain, these substances can persist through the water-treatment process and pollute waterways, harming wildlife. Hydrogen peroxide – the bleach used to lighten hair – is another everyday chemical; unlike chlorine bleach, it breaks down harmlessly when released into the environment, but can still pose health risks to both people and animals.

EACH YEAR, **CONSUMERS IN THE US** USE APPROXIMATELY

83,000 TONNES OF HAIR DYE

Fortunately, you can enjoy a new look while also caring for the planet:

- **Seek out plant-based** dyes; they can be found at more forward-thinking, eco-friendly hair salons. The colour doesn't last as long but they are better for your hair, as well as for the planet (though bear in mind that in this relatively new area there's a lot of green-washing).
- **Beware "organic"** home-dye claims: there is no regulation regarding what hair-product companies can claim to be organic. The only truly organic hair dyes are organic henna or vegetable dyes. In addition, watch out for products that claim to be "chemical-free": everything, even plants, is made up of chemicals, so this is a meaningless marketing term.
- **For relaxants**, look for products with natural ingredients such as tea tree and shea, or cleansing mud-based products. Or check online tutorials for home-made conditioners using ingredients such as coconut oil and honey.
- **Look for brands** that explain their plant-based ingredients, are proudly cruelty-free, and use eco-friendly packaging.
- **Look after your** new hair colour to help it last and avoid having to reapply it too often: use shampoos and conditioners without sulphates or sodium chloride, ingredients that will cause the colour to fade more quickly.

How bad are contact lenses for the planet?

Contact lenses might seem too small to cause a waste problem, but if incorrectly disposed of they can turn up in rivers, seas, and soil, contributing to the microplastic problem.

We get through a lot of contact lenses. In the US, for instance, around 45 million people wear them, and according to one study, 15–20% of users wash their lenses down the sink or toss them into the toilet once they have finished with them, contributing 20–23 tonnes of plastic waste a year to waterways. Lenses sink to the bottom of the sea, where they can be swallowed whole by marine life, or over time they disintegrate into microplastics (see p.96 for more on this issue).

There are other ways to get rid of disposable contact lenses and to reduce the environmental impact of using them (even though, according to one survey, 39% of lens wearers aren't sure what options are available to them). Here's how to be a more eco-friendly contact lens wearer:

- **Reduce waste** by swapping to weekly or monthly contacts rather than dailies – cutting down not only on the number of lenses but also on plastic packaging.
- **Recycle your lenses**, if you can. In the UK, a contact-lens recycling scheme allows users to send old lenses back to the manufacturer or drop them off with a local optician, so they can be recycled on a large scale. Check your lens manufacturer's website for details or ask your usual supplier what their recycling plans are.
- **If you aren't able** to recycle them, make sure lenses and packaging go in your solid waste bin rather than down the sink or loo.

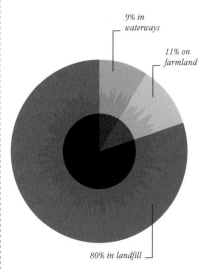

9% in waterways

11% on farmland

80% in landfill

▲ A 2018 US study investigated where contact lenses end up if they aren't recycled. Those that don't go to landfill enter bodies of water, or fields via sewage-water run-off.

Which is better, an electric toothbrush or a bamboo one?

Bamboo might seem like the most eco-friendly choice for dental hygiene, but electric toothbrushes can also be green if you know what to look for.

First things first: whatever you choose, move away from disposable plastic toothbrushes. A billion of them are thrown away every year in the US alone. Researchers reckon that almost every plastic toothbrush produced since the 1930s is still here. Being made of a mix of materials, they're almost impossible to recycle.

Returning to more natural materials is one solution to the toothbrush problem. Bamboo toothbrushes are widely available and much greener than plastic; bamboo grows quickly and needs little water to flourish.

▲ If all the toothbrushes thrown away in the US over a year were placed end to end, they would stretch around the Earth four times.

There is still no non-plastic, cruelty-free replacement for the nylon bristles, so most bamboo brushes aren't 100% biodegradable, though boar-hair bristles are an option. The handles can be commercially composted once the nylon bristles have been removed, minimizing waste. Choose responsibly sourced bamboo, and remember to compost the handles instead of sending them to landfill, to ensure they degrade quickly.

With electric toothbrushes, the situation is a little more complex. While older, battery-powered models aren't particularly eco (see p.140), newer versions can be battery-free and made of recycled plastic. They almost always have removable heads, which can be replaced every few months without the need to discard the whole toothbrush. Some companies have systems in place enabling customers to send back old toothbrush heads for recycling.

For the most sustainable option, look for electric toothbrushes that don't use removable batteries, come in plastic-free packaging, have localized supply chains (see pp.118–19), and can be recycled.

How can I have a zero-waste bathroom?

The bathroom tends to get overlooked when it comes to tackling our excessive consumption, but there are a few simple swaps you can make to help reduce, reuse, and recycle.

It's easy to see small items such as floss and cotton wool as insignificant, but when everyone thinks like this we throw away a large quantity of material made from finite resources. Several common bathroom items are downright damaging to the planet.

Wet wipes should be avoided. Widely regarded as everyday essentials for everything from removing makeup to cleaning up kids, wipes are a big single-use plastic problem. They are made of a range of materials including polyester and polypropylene, don't biodegrade, and break down into microplastics (see p.96). When disposed of down the toilet instead of in the bin, they contribute to the huge, slimy lumps of waste known as fatbergs that form in sewers.

Cotton buds are another problem. They may seem too small to do much damage, but due to the scale at which they are consumed globally, combined with the fact that they too are often flushed down the toilet, they've become a sea scourge, leading many countries to ban them.

Dental floss is often made of plastic and coated in synthetic wax and a Teflon-like substance, which stays in the environment for a long time and is toxic to humans and animals.

Being more green is about reducing your consumption however you can. Swapping to reusable items is one way individuals can make an impact; for items that can't be reused, look for biodegradable options and dispose of them appropriately.

THE UK GETS THROUGH

1.8 billion

COTTON BUDS A YEAR

- **Assess your bathroom** cabinet and see how many single-use items could be replaced with a reusable alternative.
- **Ditch the wet wipes** and replace them with reusable, washable cotton cloths or pads. If you end up using wipes as a last resort, don't flush them.
- **Swap to cotton buds** made of cardboard, and bin them after use.
- **Replace floss** with biodegradable yarn in glass jars, corn starch or bamboo versions of floss picks, or a water flosser, which uses a jet of water. For interdental brushes, choose bamboo over plastic.

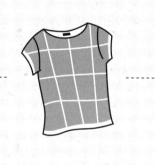

GREEN
WARDROBE

- -

Why is fast fashion such a problem?

To be more green, we have to look at how we buy, wash, and get rid of our clothes. Fast fashion might be easy and cheap for consumers, but it's terrible for the planet.

Fashion is notoriously un-eco. Simply harvesting the raw materials needed to produce all that fabric contributes to deforestation and biodiversity loss. The chemicals used in production and dyeing pollute waterways, degrade soil health, and poison factory workers. The fashion industry is one of the most polluting in the world – 70% of China's rivers and lakes are contaminated by over 11 billion litres of chemical-laden post-production water from clothing factories.

The fashion industry also uses 2% of the world's fresh water, making it the third-thirstiest industry (after oil and aviation). There are links between industrial clothing factories and desertification, as fresh water is

▲ It's hard to imagine what we would do without the fast-fashion industry, but it has created a catastrophic problem for the planet's resources.

siphoned off from lakes and rivers to irrigate cotton fields, leading to the destruction of animal populations and local weather systems. The Aral Sea in Central Asia has shrunk in size by 90% due to this practice.

The human cost

There's a big human rights issue, too. Fast-fashion brands rarely manage the factories making their clothes directly, which means they often don't oversee the working conditions. In the worst cases, women and children work unpaid overtime, there is physical and mental abuse, and wages fall well below what is required for a decent living standard.

The part we play

In addition to the human cost, it's our overconsumption – the sheer amount of stuff we buy – that is making the problem so much worse. Often our wardrobes are bulging with items.

What's more, the billions of garments that flood our stores represent enormous amounts of waste, both before and after we buy them: 60 billion square metres of textiles end up on factory floors as waste each year, and the US alone sends almost 10 million tonnes of clothing to landfill every year.

Unless attitudes change, these problems are only going to get worse. We need to produce and buy less.

While many countries are pushing for global fashion brands to hit stricter environmental targets, and some brands are self-regulating,

by banning fur and leather, and committing to using more organic, sustainable cotton, this still doesn't tackle the overconsumption issue. So, at an individual level, what can you do?

- **Buy less**. Changing our buying habits is the most effective thing we can do. Buy second-hand, go to clothes-swap events, or share between friends and siblings. Cutting back on

---

MAKING A SINGLE **PAIR OF JEANS** CAN TAKE UP TO

10,000 LITRES OF WATER

---

clothes-buying sprees reduces demand at source.

- **Invest in good-quality** clothes that won't need replacing quickly. And, when you have finished with them, keep them circulating (see p.106).
- **Support independent brands** that are open and honest about exactly how and where their clothes are made.
- **Ask questions** of your favourite global brands – without consumer pressure, they won't change.
- **Don't support brands** that mistreat the environment or their workers, and remember that big brands are only successful because we make them so. The power for change is in your pocket.

What's the issue with man-made fabrics?

Synthetic fibres make up the bulk of cheap clothes and have revolutionized our wardrobes, but they've come at a cost. There are a few things you can do to limit the negative effects.

Since the advent of synthetic fabrics in the early 20th century, clothes have become cheaper, trends have sped up exponentially, and choice has grown.

Polyester, nylon, acrylic, elastane, and spandex have enabled enormous change within the world of fashion, including giving us practical clothing such as Lycra and cosy fleeces. However, they are oil by-products, which means they are unsustainable and their manufacture releases greenhouse gases. What's more, it takes huge amounts of toxic chemicals and fresh water to produce these fabrics. The chemicals used in

---

65% OF ALL CLOTHING GLOBALLY IS MADE OF SYNTHETIC FIBRES

---

production and dyeing pollute the air and land around factories, especially those that are poorly regulated. And, when it's thrown away, synthetic clothing does not biodegrade. That's right – your ill-thought-through '70s polyester flares or '90s acrylic V-neck are still out there somewhere.

Man-made fabrics have also created a plastic problem that has seeped into every corner of the Earth: microplastics (see p.96 for more on this issue).

Recycled marine plastic can be turned into yarn (then clothes, shoes, and swimwear), which is known as Econyl, but it still sheds microplastics. Adding plastic to other materials to create complex blends also means that those clothes can't be recycled.

Semi-natural fabrics

Fabrics such as viscose, rayon, and Tencel contain a mixture of synthetic elements and plant fibres such as wood pulp and bamboo. Though often marketed as a greener choice, these fabrics nonetheless take a lot of energy, water, and trees – often from endangered forests – to produce, and the production process releases toxic chemicals into the environment.

To be green, check the label and care for fabrics appropriately:
- **Avoid buying** synthetic clothing.
- **If you do buy** something man-made, make good use of it. Aim for at least 30 wears – the recommended threshold for a garment to "work off" the emissions used to create it.

Can I help the planet by making and mending my own clothes?

Sewing your own clothes might sound daunting, but with practice anyone can do it. Mending or upcycling your clothes is a greener way to enjoy fashion.

Repairing or making clothes are great ways to avoid buying – and binning – new stuff and contributing to the global fast-fashion problem (see p.90).

Fight back by loving your clothes for longer, mending and adapting them as needed. Don't worry if you don't know how to darn, sew on a button, or take up a hem – it's never too late to learn. And your mending efforts don't have to be seamstress-level to count; there's a real move towards "visible mending" amongst many green sewers.

- **"Repair cafés"** are free spaces where volunteers will teach you sewing or darning skills. Small-scale sewing workshops and classes are seeing a massive rise in interest in many parts of the world.
- **Watch online videos** with step-by-step tutorials on essential mending skills such as darning.
- **Subscribe to an online** sewing magazine for patterns, tips, and guidance on sewing skills.
- **Try making** your own clothes from scratch. You are much more likely to treasure something you've made yourself, and keep it for far longer, than something that you bought cheaply from a global

brand. Make your new hobby greener by using fabric offcuts and clever waste-reducing patterns (there are plenty online), or buy patterns and material from small-scale, sustainably focused fashion designers.

- **Join an evening class** to learn the basics, or improve your skills, or set up your own sewing group with like-minded friends, where you can swap skills and discuss projects.

KEEPING YOUR CLOTHES IN CIRCULATION FOR JUST **9 MORE MONTHS** WOULD REDUCE THEIR **CARBON FOOTPRINT BY UP TO 30%**

Which natural fabrics are the most eco-friendly?

It's not as straightforward as "natural is good, man-made is bad" – natural fabrics have their own environmental issues. Considering each fabric's life cycle can help you make decisions.

Any material made from plants or animal by-products is "natural". The most common examples are cotton, linen (which is made from the flax plant), hemp, silk, and bamboo, along with leather (see p.102) and wool. Natural materials don't shed microplastics (see p.96), and they biodegrade at the end of their life. They are also often antibacterial, and they regulate your body temperature in the heat and cold, leading to less sweat; this means you don't have to wash them as often as synthetic materials, saving water and energy.

However, there are still certain environmental concerns with natural fabrics. For every ethical choice, there's often a further consequence. No material has zero impact.

Ultimately, the greenest option is to make good use of the clothes that you have now. If the fabrics currently in your wardrobe aren't the most sustainably produced, don't feel you need to throw them out and start again. Look after your clothes, and, when you do need to invest in a new item, choose a more eco-friendly fabric.

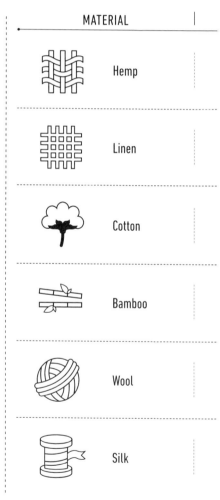

MATERIAL	
	Hemp
	Linen
	Cotton
	Bamboo
	Wool
	Silk

Comparing natural fabrics

It's impossible to give a definitive ranking of natural fabrics from best to worst. Each one has an impact of some kind, but factors such as how easy the crop is to grow, whether harsh chemicals are involved in the production, and how long the finished clothes will last all affect how eco-friendly they can be.

PROS	CONS
The most efficient fibre crop: grows almost anywhere on very little water and nutrients; produces 250% more fabric per land area, than cotton using 50% less water. Stops soil erosion and doesn't need pesticides. Durable and breathable, so needs less washing.	*Tends to wrinkle, and can take a while to wear in. Doesn't hold bold colours well.*
Breathable, reduces sweating (so needs washing less often), dries quickly, and lasts a long time. The second-most efficient fibre crop: the whole plant is used, and it can be grown in soil that isn't suitable for food.	*It takes a relatively long time to turn the raw fibres into a yarn, so it is expensive to produce and buy. Crumples easily, and can shrink easily if not correctly washed.*
Biodegrades easily, and doesn't require a complex chemical process to be transformed into a durable fabric. Organic crops are grown in pesticide-free soil, which is a more water-efficient process.	*Incredibly water-reliant, and mostly grown in arid areas, diverting water from other sources. Non-organic uses large quantities of pesticides; only 1% is organic. Look for the Global Organic Textile Standard (GOTS).*
Grows quickly, doesn't need pesticides, and uses a lot less water than cotton – it also costs less to produce, and creates a hard-wearing fabric.	*There's usually no guarantee it's being grown sustainably, and it requires an intensive process to produce; most of the resultant chemical waste goes into the environment.*
Naturally antibacterial, moisture-wicking, and temperature-regulating, meaning it can keep you warm and cool. A long-lasting material that doesn't need much washing and can be washed cold.	*Commercial sheep farms have a worse eco-impact than many synthetic materials (see pp.36–37). Cheap wool often comes from farms where animal cruelty is rife (look for the Responsible Wool Standard for ethical wool).*
Undyed or naturally dyed silks are available (look for GOTS-certified products). "Peace silk" is processed without killing the silkworms, and artificial silk (called spider silk) is just as strong but is made from wheat, yeast, and sugar.	*Some silks are produced with chemicals and use toxic dyes. Most commercial silkworm farms kill the worm to extract the threads that are woven into silk, so it is not considered vegan.*

How can I stop microplastics from my clothes getting into the sea?

Microplastics have been found in every corner of our planet. A large proportion comes from clothes, and we can play a role in reducing them.

When items of clothing made from synthetic materials rub together in the drum of a washing machine, friction causes tiny bits of plastic yarn to break off and wash away in the water. These are microplastics: tiny fibres less than 5mm in length, too small to be caught by filters in your washing machine or at sewage works. They now exist in water systems, icebergs, fish, and food, and have been found on every square metre of coastline and at every depth of the oceans.

Coated in chemicals – many of which are toxic to the animals that unwittingly consume them – these fibres are geared to last. That's great if you want a fleece coat to last you a decade, but not so fantastic when the microplastics are polluting the Earth and entering the food chain.

Acrylic releases the most fibres, over 1.5 times more than polyester, and 5 times more than a polyester-cotton mix. Washing clothes on a delicate cycle has been found to be even worse for releasing microfibres

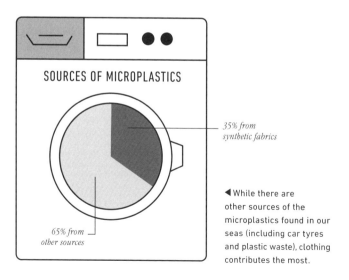

SOURCES OF MICROPLASTICS

35% from synthetic fabrics

65% from other sources

◀ While there are other sources of the microplastics found in our seas (including car tyres and plastic waste), clothing contributes the most.

than a normal one, probably because the higher water volume used pushes more fibres out of the fabric.

So now you know the scope, what can you do to reduce the massive issue of microplastics?

- **Invest in an** in-wash laundry bag or ball that catches microplastics; these are made from an incredibly fine mesh, through which the particles can't escape.
- **Swap to natural fabrics** where you can (see p.94).
- **Wash your clothes less** often whenever possible (see right).
- **When you do wash** them, make sure you fill the machine,

A **SINGLE LOAD** OF WASHING CAN RELEASE MORE THAN

700,000 MICRO-FIBRES

---

to reduce friction so fewer fibres are shed. Doing more cold-water washing and avoiding the tumble dryer (see p.99) will also help reduce the number of microplastics released by your clothes.

- **If you're looking** for a new washing machine, choose one that comes with a built-in microplastic filter, or buy one as an add-on to your existing machine.

How often should I wash my clothes?

Good news! One of the easiest things you can do to help the environment is simply to wash your clothes less.

Less laundry means less energy used, less detergent (see p.98), and fewer microplastics washed into the ocean. Rather than shoving everything in the drum after one wear, take a bit more care over your clothes. Putting them away rather than leaving them lying around will help them last longer between washes.

While it goes without saying that some items, such as underwear, really need to be washed after each wear, others might not need a clean as often as you think:

- **Natural materials** need less washing than synthetic fabrics (see p.94). When washing wool or silk, use a lower temperature (30°C) and a delicate cycle, to save energy and avoid damaging the fabric.
- **For small stains**, spot-washing (scrubbing the area clean by hand) is greener than washing the whole garment.
- **As for jeans**, denim fans advise going as long as you can between washes. When you do wash your jeans, do it by hand in cold water, then hang them to dry, to help them last longer.

What's the greenest way to do my laundry?

Forget pods and cupfuls of liquid detergent: reusable options that can be disposed of responsibly once used up will lessen your environmental impact – and save money too.

Laundry has a big impact on the planet. The average American household does 400 loads of washing a year. Each wash can get through up to 182 litres of water (top-loading washing machines use more than front-loaders), and 75–90% of the energy a washing machine uses is to heat the water.

Mainstream detergents contain several damaging substances: phosphates (which disrupt eco-systems), bleach, petrochemicals, palm oil, and sodium lauryl sulphate (SLS). Liquid detergent and laundry pods also come in plastic bottles, tubs, and pouches, which are often unrecyclable.

The alternative is eco-friendly products that use plant-based ingredients, and don't come covered in single-use plastic.

Eco eggs are plastic eggs filled with natural mineral pellets. When mixed with hot water, these react to lift dirt out of fabric and soften clothes. They don't contain any harsh chemicals, so can be good for sensitive skin. Each pellet mix lasts for around 70 washes.

Another option is soap nuts. You place them in a cotton bag and throw them in with your washing, where the hot water causes them to release saponin, a natural soap-like chemical, which combats dirt and stains. The nuts can be reused

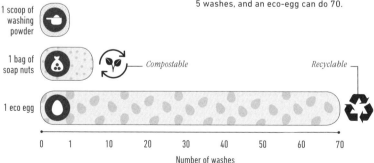

▼ While mainstream detergent can't be reused, soap nuts will last approximately 5 washes, and an eco-egg can do 70.

1 scoop of washing powder

1 bag of soap nuts — Compostable

1 eco egg — Recyclable

0 1 10 20 30 40 50 60 70

Number of washes

several times. They have been used in India for centuries, although some people are sceptical about their efficacy. They won't work on slow or cold washes, but they are cost-effective, plastic-packaging-free, and easily found online.

If you don't want to move away from traditional detergents entirely, ditch the pods and go back to washing powder. Look for biodegradable and/or plant-based versions. Choose detergent in cardboard packaging and buy it in bulk, or choose refills – a zero-waste store would be a good place to look (see p.115 for more information on

80% OF OUR CLOTHING'S TOTAL ECO-IMPACT IS FROM LAUNDERING IT

these). You can replace fabric conditioner with white vinegar for another natural approach.

To cut down on energy use, see if you can do more cold- or hand-washing. Some items, such as delicates and jeans, don't mind a cold rinse. You can also cut down on how often you wash certain types of garment (see p.97).

What's the best way to dry my clothes?

It's time to go back to traditional ways of drying clothes – the planet and your purse will thank you.

While you might love the warm softness of tumble-dried towels, they are bad news for the planet. Used in 75% of American households, dryers are one of the most energy-hungry appliances we own. The average tumble dryer produces 1.8.kg of CO_2 each time it is used – which quickly adds up.

Tumble-drying also creates friction between clothes, causing synthetic fabrics to shed microplastics, which end up in our seas (see p.96). Of all of the microplastics in the oceans, 35% originate from synthetic clothes, and are released via washing machines and clothes dryers.

There are a lot of complicated issues in this book, but this isn't one of them. Switch to air-drying, either using a clothes rack indoors, or a clothes line if you have a garden or balcony, provided your local area doesn't prohibit them (and if they do, write to members of local government asking for the rule to be revoked!). It's not just the Earth you'll be helping, it's your pocket too – clothes dryers are expensive to run.

"Total clothing consumption is projected to rise *by 63% in the next decade.*"

Can I be green and have my clothes dry-cleaned?

The dreaded "dry-clean only" label often means high prices and inconvenience, but it also comes with consequences for our water supply, and can impact on human health.

In short, no. There is nothing green about most dry-cleaning. Even if your dry-cleaner now uses biodegradable plastic to cover your clean, pressed clothes, the chances are that the cleaning process itself hasn't changed.

Dry-cleaning isn't actually "dry"; it's simply called that because it doesn't use water. For decades, the process has involved the use of perchloroethylene (known as perc), a chemical that can damage the environment as well as causing cancer in humans. It also produces hazardous waste that can leach into water supplies if not properly contained. Perc isn't as common globally as it once was, but it is still widely used in many countries. And in some cases, companies wishing to avoid perc have simply switched to other toxic solvents.

If your garment says "dry-clean only", look for "wet-cleaning" dry-cleaners, a green alternative that washes with water rather than man-made chemicals. Or seek out services that use liquid carbon dioxide as the cleaning solvent. It's not actually as polluting as it might sound. This is the same stuff that carbonates fizzy drinks; these companies use CO_2 that is a by-product of other industries, and it's reused for multiple washes.

In addition to the issue of the chemical processes, dry-cleaning also contributes to the coat-hanger industry: 8–10 billion coat hangers are made and thrown away each year. Both plastic and metal coat hangers are difficult to recycle, so usually end up in landfill.

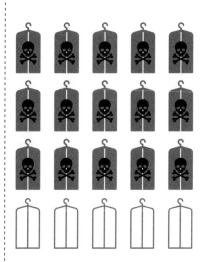

▲ In India, a survey showed that 75% of dry-cleaned garments tested had perc on them.

Is vegan leather more eco-friendly than real leather?

*Not everything vegan has less of an impact on the planet.
It often comes down to personal choice; a matter of weighing
up all the issues to find a solution that fits your values.*

Real leather has a lot of negatives, from issues around animal welfare to the chemicals used in tanning and dyeing. Often, leather is treated with chemicals such as chromium and aldehydes, contributing to the pollution of waterways. Sometimes, though, there are no easy sustainable swaps, and this applies to leather.

"Vegan leather" might sound like a great replacement, but it isn't anything new: also known as "pleather", it was first invented not for ethical reasons but as a cheap alternative to real leather. It doesn't contain animal products, but it's still not great for the environment. Most vegan leather is made using either polyurethane (PU), or polyvinyl chloride (PVC), both of which are plastics that undergo complex toxic processes to become a leather-like material. Being synthetic, these materials don't biodegrade.

The laminated surface can quickly crack, and items often end up in landfill. Real leather is longer-lasting.

FAUX-LEATHER
SHOES LAST FOR
1 or 2 YEARS ON AVERAGE

ANIMAL-LEATHER
SHOES, WHEN WELL
CARED-FOR, CAN LAST
FOR **A LIFETIME**

▲ The damaging aspects of a pair of shoes' manufacture must be weighed against how long they will last, being frequently worn.

It's easier to mend, it biodegrades, and it is often a by-product of the meat and dairy industries.

Some faux-leather manufacturers are greener than others (in EU countries, ask if they're compliant with REACH, a chemical-industry regulation), but few fashion brands are transparent about their supply chains. There are exceptions: some ethical brands make sure their vegan leather is made with recycled polyester and is solvent-free, though this does push the price up.

25% OF THE **SYNTHETIC CHEMICALS** PRODUCED WORLDWIDE ARE USED **TO MAKE TEXTILES**

There is also a growing range of fruit- and vegetable-derived vegan leathers, made from mushrooms, apples, rhubarb, and more. This has a lower eco-impact than faux leather. Piñatex, made from pineapple fibres, is popular for its metallic finish.

For eco-friendly real leather, some brands make products out of offcuts that would otherwise be thrown away. They also use vegetable dyes, employ craftspeople, and offset the energy used in production with renewables.

Your choice depends on your values and what environmental issue you want to prioritize. The greenest options are either to avoid all kinds of leather, or to buy second-hand.

How bad for the planet are sequins?

A bit of sparkle might make you look fabulous, but it's a problem for the seas.

Sequins are usually made of PVC plastic, in a process that creates a lot of plastic waste. PVC contains phthalates, chemicals that can upset hormonal systems in animals and humans if they enter the food chain.

When they come loose from clothes (often in the wash), these tiny, shiny discs pollute the soil and waterways, with many getting washed into the ocean, where fish mistake them for food. Their composition and small size mean that they can't be recycled. The irony is that sequinned clothes are often the items we get the least wear out of, yet all that plastic will still be around in centuries to come.

All of the above eco-doom is also true for glitter (sorry to spoil the party).

If you've already got a sequinned number or two in the cupboard, keep them in circulation, rather than throwing them away. There are biodegradable sequins and glitter available, but most of these still contain a small amount of plastic, so your best bet is to avoid them, too. You can still be fabulous without shiny bits of plastic.

Are there eco-friendly glasses and sunglasses?

Glasses might not be the first thing that come to mind when you think about being eco, but adjusting every purchase in your life – even this one – can have an impact.

Three-quarters of people in the developed world wear glasses, and even more wear sunglasses, but have you ever thought about glasses' environmental impact?

Glasses tend to be made up of multiple materials (including metals such as aluminium and titanium, and plastic), which makes them difficult to process at recycling facilities. Most cheap sunglasses, meanwhile, are 100% plastic and are discarded quickly, usually adding to landfill waste. Here's what to do for sustainable specs:

- **Avoid acetate**, a material derived from wood pulp, which, though labelled "sustainable", is often produced in unregulated factories using toxic substances. Acetate frames can't be recycled like plastic or wooden ones. "Bio-acetate" is available, and does biodegrade, but even the manufacturers don't know how long that takes.
- **Look for natural** or recycled materials such as sustainably sourced wood, bamboo, recycled plastic, or even 3D-printed frames made from scraps of car dashboard or old fridge plastic.
- **Buy from companies** that give back – some use revenue to fund educational programmes, or for restoring-vision initiatives. Some brands allow you to return glasses or sunglasses to be given to people in need.
- **Recycle your glasses** once they're no longer wearable. Plastic and glass lenses can be put in with in your normal recycling.

✓ Sustainable bamboo

✓ Recycled plastic

✓ Metal

✕ Acetate

✕ Unrecycled plastic

▲ Prioritize natural and recycled materials with clear supply chains over new and unsustainable substances.

How can I make sure my jewellery is sustainable?

If you want to adorn yourself without harming the planet, thinking about the sustainability of the materials used and how these were extracted can help you make greener choices.

Cheap jewellery is often made of plastic or metal alloys. These items are poorly made and quick to discolour, and tend to end up in landfill rather than being reused and recycled.

Silver and gold are longer-lasting, but check where they come from. Most mining for precious metals uses toxic extraction methods, causes deforestation, contaminates the soil and air, and harms wildlife. The industry also has a terrible human-rights record. Of all the gold mined globally, almost 50% is destined to end up as jewellery. Most of that comes from small-scale mines, where workers (some of whom are children) have only basic tools, and are in contact with poisonous substances such as mercury. Be wary of gemstones, too, which rarely have a clear supply chain; they are often mined unsustainably in dangerous working conditions.

Being green with jewellery means choosing carefully and making it last.

- **For everyday jewellery**, avoid the high street and look for pieces made locally. Consider wooden, bamboo, or upcycled options: earrings made from bicycle inner tubes, necklaces from knotted T-shirt yarn, bracelets from cut-up bouncy castles – the possibilities are almost endless!

- **If you're buying** gold or silver, look for Fairtrade or Fairmined certifications, which guarantee that they were mined ethically. Only around 1% of the world's supply is certified as such. Alternatively, buy

USING **RECYCLED MATERIALS** COULD CUT THE ECO-IMPACT OF **JEWELLERY PRODUCTION** BY **95%**

recycled gold or silver, so you're not using virgin materials.

- **Choose lab-grown** diamonds and gems; they are chemically identical to natural rocks, but don't have the same ecological impact and cost a fraction of the price. Or buy from designers who are open about how and where they source gemstones.

- **Look after jewellery**. Store it safely and keep it away from water to prolong its life.

- **Donate or resell** old jewellery, or, if it's no longer wearable, recycle it – there are various organizations and charities that will accept it.

Why is it important to recycle clothes?

Your clothes take a huge amount of resources to create, ship, and sell – being green means doing everything you can to avoid binning them.

In the last couple of decades the amount of clothes we buy has doubled. Over 80 billion garments are made worldwide every year, using vast quantities of energy, raw materials, chemicals, labour, and water – it takes 3,000 litres of water to make just one cotton shirt (see p.90 for more on this).

Since we definitely don't *need* all those clothes, many of them get quickly discarded. In the US, about 36kg of clothing is thrown away per person, each year. We don't recycle anywhere near enough – in the UK, 41% of people are unsure of how to recycle clothes. Clothes that aren't recycled end up in landfill or burnt, emitting toxic fumes from the chemicals used in their manufacture.

One of the easiest ways to be greener is to value your clothes and

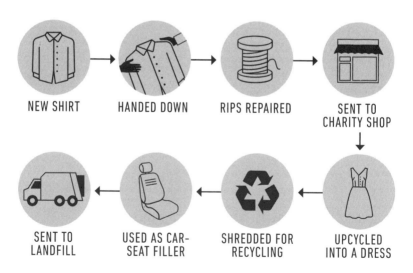

NEW SHIRT → HANDED DOWN → RIPS REPAIRED → SENT TO CHARITY SHOP

SENT TO LANDFILL ← USED AS CAR-SEAT FILLER ← SHREDDED FOR RECYCLING ← UPCYCLED INTO A DRESS

▲ A garment's life doesn't have to end when you stop wearing it – it can be reused by others and recycled for new purposes.

make the best possible use of them. That applies both while they're in your wardrobe, and after they've left it.

Where clothes are concerned, "recycling" simply means allowing them to carry on being useful after

---

OF ALL THE **CLOTHES WE DISCARD** WORLDWIDE, ONLY **20%** ARE **REUSED** OR **RECYCLED**

---

you have finished using them, by donating or selling them, or sending them off to be made into new items.

Extending the life of your clothes reduces the impact of the energy and resources used to make them, since you avoid replacing them with new items. What's more, it means someone else will wear the clothes, rather than buying new.

If your clothes are no longer wearable, it's well worth dropping them off at a clothes bank or other clothes recycling facility. From here, they can be resold as filler for car seats and other lower-grade textile products. Think of clothes as having different life stages – so, rather than a straight line from factory to shop, to wardrobe to bin, they are mended, upcycled, adjusted, passed on, or repurposed.

How do you recycle shoes?

There's a difference between recycling shoes that can still be worn and those that are past it.

Take any shoes that are in a wearable condition to shoe banks or second-hand clothes shops, or give them to local schemes donating shoes to those in need or to international programmes that deliver specific types of shoes to people who need them (for instance, hiking boots for sherpas in Nepal).

Considering how many shoes we get through (it's been reported that 300 million pairs a year are thrown away in the US), there's a severe lack of recycling options for those that are no longer wearable. While a satisfactory answer is still out of reach, there are a few things you can do:

- **Buy from brands** that recycle their own products if you send them back.
- **Buy higher-quality shoes**. Invest in shoes that you love, that will last, and that can be mended, rather than fast-fashion shoes that only last a season.
- **Get worn-out shoes** repaired.
- **Choose shoes that** are plastic-free, sustainably made, or biodegradable, so that even if they end up in landfill, you're lowering their long-term impact.

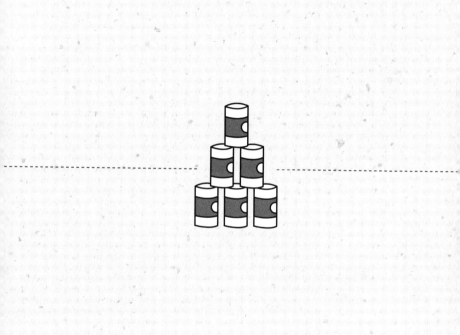

GREEN
SHOPPING

What's the greenest way to shop for food?

Week in, week out, after work or at the weekends, food shopping is an important part of life. Where – and how – you do it makes a difference.

Big supermarkets are, for many of us, a fixture of everyday life, but they are linked to a number of planet-harming practices. In order to supply a wide range of produce all year round for huge numbers of customers, supermarkets have had to develop complex global supply chains (see pp.118–19 for more on the significance of these). Supermarkets rely heavily on plastic, preservatives, and processed foods, all of which are bad news for the environment.

Then there are the buildings themselves. Supermarkets use up vast amounts of energy, with large fridges and freezer units as well as lighting, heating, and air conditioning.

There's also the issue of food waste: supermarkets are responsible for enormous amounts of fresh-food wastage, rejecting produce from farmers and suppliers. For instance, 19% of all lettuces never make it to consumers. Overall, £1 billion worth of food is grown and wasted per year

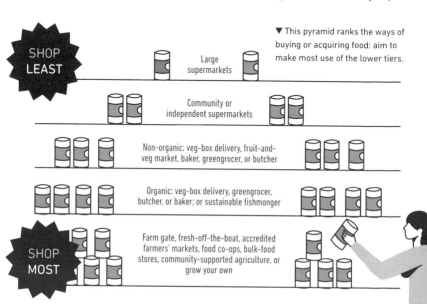

▼ This pyramid ranks the ways of buying or acquiring food: aim to make most use of the lower tiers.

SHOP LEAST

Large supermarkets

Community or independent supermarkets

Non-organic: veg-box delivery, fruit-and-veg market, baker, greengrocer, or butcher

Organic: veg-box delivery, greengrocer, butcher, or baker; or sustainable fishmonger

SHOP MOST

Farm gate, fresh-off-the-boat, accredited farmers' markets, food co-ops, bulk-food stores, community-supported agriculture, or grow your own

in the UK without ever reaching the supermarket shelves, and the quality demanded by supermarkets is a key reason for this problem.

Positive change

The good news is that some people in the industry are already attempting to leave this unsustainable system behind. The UK's supermarkets signed a pledge in 2019 to reduce their food waste by 50% by 2030, while some supermarkets in Australia are aiming

---

THE UK'S SUPERMARKETS
PRODUCED MORE THAN

800,000 TONNES OF

PLASTIC WASTE IN 2018

---

to achieve this target sooner. More and more supermarkets are selling "wonky" or non-perfect fruit and veg that would previously have been rejected, and many are working harder at redistributing food to food banks or charities instead of binning it. But more can be done: in France, for instance, legislation has been passed banning supermarkets from throwing out edible food.

Supermarkets in many countries are also becoming greener in their infrastructure, with big, out-of-town supermarkets powered by solar, using LED lights, and providing charging points for electric vehicles (which can be made greener by storing and discharging excess energy from renewable resources such as solar panels on the building's roof). Imagine if your supermarket was self-sufficient in energy and a hub of green technology.

At an individual level, there are plenty of things you can do to reduce the environmental impact of food shopping:

- **Support farmers'** markets, local zero-waste shops, and farm shops as much as you can. Aside from the reduction in plastic packaging, supporting local supply chains help builds a more resilient local economy.

- **If you need to** drive to get to the shops, try to do just one weekly shop, to minimize emission-heavy travelling. If you can walk or cycle to the shops, of course, it makes no difference how often you go, so do whatever works best to keep your household fed while avoiding food waste (see pp.26–27 for more on this).

- **Consider getting** your groceries delivered as an alternative to driving to the shop – if your supermarket uses electric delivery vans, even better!

- **Buy ingredients** in bulk, to reduce the amount of plastic you'll go home with.

- **Say no to paper receipts**: they are made of more than one type of material (they use heat, not ink, to print the details), meaning they aren't recyclable. Opt for digital receipts when possible, instead.

Which are greener – paper, plastic, or cotton bags?

When it comes to carrying your shopping home, there's bagloads of information to unpack. Plastic-free isn't always greener – the key issue is how many times a bag will be used in its lifetime.

There are plenty of reasons to avoid single-use plastic carrier bags: they are manufactured from oil, a rapidly depleting fossil fuel; they are rarely recycled – globally we use 5 trillion a year and only recycle around 1%; once discarded, they break down into microplastics (see p.96), which enter waterways and travel up food chains; and many end up in our oceans – over 100,000 marine animals die each year as a result of eating them (one in three leatherback turtles has a plastic bag in its stomach).

It's common sense to avoid single-use plastic bags at all costs, but when you look closely at the alternatives, things get a bit more complicated. To decide how green a bag is, we need to consider its whole life cycle: the resources used in its production, how much energy went

PAPER BAG
4
USES

REUSABLE PLASTIC BAG
12 USES

TOTE BAG
130
USES

▲ "Greener" bags need to be used multiple times in order to have less impact than single-use plastic.

into making it, how long it lasts, whether it can be recycled, and what it breaks down into once discarded.

Paper bags take four times the energy needed to produce a plastic bag. Being heavier than plastic, they also cause more transportation emissions, and unless they are made of sustainably sourced wood, their manufacture leads to deforestation. Taking all the factors into account, a paper bag is greener than plastic as long as it's made from sustainable wood and used at least four times.

A cotton tote bag, meanwhile, needs to be used more than 130 times to be more efficient than plastic, in terms of both the resources and energy used to make it. On the plus side, though, bags made from natural fibres such as cotton don't cause pollution when disposed of. A traditional string bag is a good choice – it uses fewer resources to make than a tote bag, scrunches up small enough to be carried in a pocket or handbag, and is incredibly durable.

Reusable plastic bags are often much worse than thin single-use versions – see right for more on this. To be a greener bag user, the key is to use as few as possible, whatever the material:

- **Use the bag you already** have, whether it be paper, plastic, or cotton, and keep using it for as long as you possibly can.
- **Remember to take** your reusable bag out with you – it's all too easy to end up with a mountain of bags cluttering up your home or car.

Is a bag for life really an eco-friendly choice?

A sturdy plastic reusable bag is presented as a green option, but how much use will you really get out of it?

Many countries are discouraging the use of single-use plastic carrier bags – in the UK, for instance, a tax has resulted in a 40% reduction in the number of bags found on beaches. Many supermarkets no longer provide single-use bags; instead, they offer a reusable "bag for life" that can be replaced for free when it wears out. But these heavier, stronger bags use more plastic and cause more emissions when manufactured; so unless you use one more than 12 times, it's actually worse for the planet than its

---

40% OF SHOPPERS IN THE US SAY THEY **REGULARLY FORGET** TO TAKE A REUSABLE BAG TO THE SHOPS

---

single-use predecessor. In the US, these bags are currently only used around three times on average – so, for now at least, they are not the dream solution that environmentalists and governments hoped for.

Should I choose products in glass or metal containers rather than plastic?

When choosing between items in different kinds of packaging, think less about the material itself and more about whether you will be able to extend the life of the container by reusing it.

Pretty much anything you are going to reuse is better for the planet than single-use plastic. Plastics come from an unsustainable source, they cause extensive pollution, and they degrade each time they are recycled. Avoid black plastic at all costs. The machines at most recycling facilities can't detect it on the conveyor belt, so it goes straight to landfill (see p.24).

"Plant-based" plastics, also known as bioplastics, might sound green, but unless they are disposed of in industrial composting facilities they will break down into harmful microplastics in just the same way as regular plastic.

MAKING CANS FROM **RECYCLED ALUMINIUM** RATHER THAN NEW METAL USES **95%** **LESS ENERGY**

Metal and glass are easy to recycle. If you buy something in glass because you'll reuse the jar to store something else in, or refill it, that's even better.

However, it's not always advisable, or even possible, to choose glass or metal packaging instead of plastic. The types of plastic that can be recycled will vary depending on

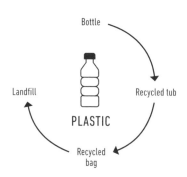

▲ Plastic becomes less versatile each time it's recycled, so its life cycle is often short.

▲ Glass doesn't lose quality when recycled, so can be reused and repurposed endlessly.

where you live, so it's worth doing some research to identify what sorts will definitely be going to landfill. With any kind of packaging, we should consider how it was made, whether it was made with recycled materials, how it was transported, and how and where it will be disposed of. Metal, glass, and plastic all have pros and cons in different parts of their life cycle – no packaging is completely eco-friendly.

Take soft drinks, for instance: your first choice should be an aluminium can if it's made from recycled metal, rather than a glass bottle (which takes more energy to transport), but prioritize both of those over a plastic bottle. If you buy glass or metal, make sure you really do recycle it. The production of these bottles is often more emission-heavy than that of plastic; recycling them avoids new ones having to be made from scratch, reducing CO_2 emissions.

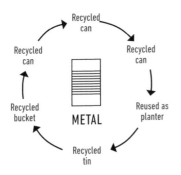

▲ Common metals such as aluminium and steel can also be recycled indefinitely.

How does a zero-waste shop work?

The explosion of zero-waste shops is a welcome change from wasteful, emission-heavy supermarkets.

A zero-waste (or bulk food) store stocks loose dry goods and often cleaning products, so you can weigh out or fill up your own containers with what you need. Most also sell containers or provide ones you can return, or have paper bags for dry goods. You pay by weight, which reduces the need for excessive amounts of packaging (for both you and the shop). Because of this, prices are often lower – packaging can add around 7% to the prices of supermarket items. Furthermore, you're investing in shorter supply chains, meaning the food has had less distance to travel.

Most zero-waste shops also sell locally sourced fruit and vegetables, bread, and eggs, as well as plastic-free household essentials such as beeswax wraps and bamboo toothbrushes. It's hard to beat the satisfaction of weighing out exactly the amount you need, or refilling old plastic bottles to save them from landfill. And don't forget that you'll be supporting a local business, which keeps your hard-earned cash working in your area.

Which is greener, online shopping or a bricks-and-mortar shop?

The eco-impact of your shopping depends a lot on how you go about it. When you have a choice between buying something in-store or online, there are several factors to consider.

How to do your shopping in the greenest possible way is a complex conundrum, but the key points to focus on are energy, fuels, and packaging.

Energy and fuel

A physical shop uses more energy than an online store – shops need to be lit, heated, and air-conditioned in order to provide a comfortable environment for customers. Driving yourself to the shops uses up non-renewable fuel and generates emissions. However, if you shop locally, you could walk, cycle, or use public transport. An online store's delivery van is more fuel-efficient than a car, because it transports dozens of items at once, reducing the number of journeys needed to get the goods to customers. Go one better and find brands that deliver with electric vehicles or carbon-offset their journeys. Research shows that if we all shopped exclusively online, there would be a 35% reduction in energy used and CO_2 emissions. However, this figure assumes we *all* move away from *all* physical stores, which is not feasible, at least in the short or medium term. Looking at long-term trends, it's clear that while e-commerce is expanding worldwide, pre-2020 our visits to physical shops hadn't decreased by the same amount – which means that we have been shopping more than ever, in both physical and virtual stores.

Packaging

While shoppers are using fewer single-use plastic carrier bags, the increase in deliveries of online orders results in a huge amount more packaging, including bubble

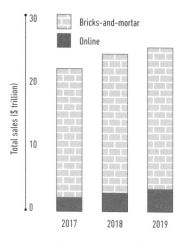

▲ Shopping has increased worldwide – and so have its negative environmental effects.

wrap, padded envelopes, plastic parcel bags, and foam chips. One report, which looked at online shopping trends in 17 countries, found that the average person in Beijing now receives 70 parcels a year – and with such figures rising, packaging is responsible

---

THE **AVERAGE CAR JOURNEY** TO AND FROM A SHOP GENERATES

24 TIMES **THE CO$_2$** OF THE AVERAGE DELIVERY FROM AN **ONLINE SHOP**

---

for more and more emissions and pollution. Look out for online brands with proactive policies on waste management, or that use recycled or recyclable cardboard packaging.

Greener shopping

Whether you shop online or on the high street, don't buy goods that have to travel thousands of miles – choose shops with shorter supply chains. Online, buy from as few different sources as possible, and consolidate your orders to reduce the amount of packaging and posted parcels. Avoid returning items, too (see right). Above all, buy less. The greenest option of all is to reduce the amount you consume, however you buy it.

What's the problem with online returns?

It's easier than ever to send items back when you shop online – but your free returns aren't free for the planet.

One of the most convenient aspects of online shopping is how easy it is to return things. For many of us, it's become normal to order lots of items and send most of them back, with some shoppers making a habit of ordering items of clothing to wear once and return. In Australia, for instance, there are two million online purchase parcels delivered every day; of those that contain clothing, one in three are returned. In some parts of the developed world, the return rate for clothes bought online is nearly 50%.

All those extra delivery vehicles on the roads, plus the large volume of parcels being flown internationally, means a big increase in CO$_2$ emissions. What's more, many returned items are not resold but are sent straight to landfill – it's often more profitable than going to the effort of repackaging them.

Reducing your impact means avoiding returns whenever you can. Buy items that you are likely to need to return in a physical shop, and make returning an item the exception, not the norm.

Why is a shorter supply chain more eco-friendly?

With supply chains, less is more: the fewer steps needed to manufacture a product and get it to you, the better it is for the planet.

A supply chain is every step taken to create a product from scratch and deliver it to the consumer. In the last hundred years, supply chains have become ever more complex, as global companies take advantage of cheap labour and raw materials, as well as tax incentives offered by different countries. Often, food or goods are produced in one country, processed in another, and packaged in yet another. Shorter supply chains are essential for long-term sustainability, for a number of reasons.

Avoiding waste

Shorter supply chains reduce waste, especially in the food industry. In the

---

90% OF THE AVERAGE COMPANY'S **ECO-IMPACT** COMES FROM **ITS SUPPLY CHAINS**

US and Canada, for example, 40% of food is wasted along the supply chain, due to factors such as inadequate storage, damage in transit, or bad stock management. Globally, the food that's wasted

before it gets to consumers could feed half the world's population. With fewer steps from field to fork, there's less opportunity for waste and more connection with producers. Knowing that something was produced by identifiable people often makes us value it more, which in turn makes us less likely to waste it.

Reducing packaging and emissions

Packaging can be reduced when the supply chain is shorter. Enormous quantities of plastic are used in the long-distance transportation of foods, to minimize damage and maintain freshness. In contrast, food that has only a short distance to travel can be kept in non-plastic, minimal packaging. More and more shops and restaurants are asking their local suppliers to keep packaging to a minimum, and many are finding inventive ways to reuse containers, rather than simply unloading goods and binning the packaging.

In addition, the reduced travel distance that comes with shorter supply chains mean fewer emissions from transport vehicles. Commercial shipping is responsible for 2.1% of all

▼ The more links in a product's supply chain, the harder it is to keep track of its carbon footprint.

Farm

Supermarket   Factory   Distributor   Farm

This complex supply chain could have many more steps along it

Bakery   Flour mill   Farm

CO_2 emissions worldwide, as well as increasing marine pollution and disrupting ocean ecosystems.

Supporting local businesses

Money stays in your locality when supply chains are shorter, and this brings a variety of benefits. Business owners who feel personally invested in their local area are more inclined to support initiatives that improve the environment for everyone – and that increases the number of new businesses, who employ more people, who then invest back into the local economy.

What's more, research has shown that we're happier when we have stronger connections to our community. Shorter supply chains bring the human element back into business and retail, which has been lost by globalization and outsourcing over many decades. Enterprises such as zero-waste shops offer customers and staff the opportunity to discuss and learn more about how food and other goods are produced, transported, and sold – as well as how to be proactive in making supply chains more sustainable.

Accountability

Accountability is another key advantage – knowing the people in your supply chain makes it easier to hold people to account and raise standards if necessary. In some global industries, such as fast fashion (see pp. 90–91), supply chains have become so complex and opaque that we consumers have no idea where our clothes were made, by whom, or under what conditions, making it harder to push for a greener industry.

How can I choose the greenest furniture for my home?

Furnishing your house in an eco-friendly way means three things: getting your tools out, buying secondhand, and choosing sustainable materials.

Being green means questioning your need before you buy. Can you mend or upcycle something you already have? If not, why limit your search to brand new products? Say hello to secondhand stores and online marketplaces, and embrace the maxim "one person's trash is another's treasure". The thrill of finding a perfect pre-loved piece is hard to beat.

If you're sure you need to buy new furniture, it's crucial to do your research into where, and from what, it was made. Furniture made from virgin materials takes a lot of energy

---

18% OF FORESTS ARE PROTECTED; THE OTHER 82% ARE AT RISK OF BEING DESTROYED

---

to create and ship. What's more, many types of wood are sourced unsustainably, through deforestation and illegal logging. If you're buying wooden furniture, make sure you are not unwittingly supporting the abuse of indigenous peoples' land and the destruction of wildlife habitats.

Opt for sustainably grown wood – the Forest Stewardship Certification (FSC) logo on wooden items guarantees that they were responsibly sourced. Or go for bamboo or other natural, non-precious materials.

Buying handmade furniture from a local craftsperson is a good option, as you won't need to worry about the emissions caused by its production and transportation. Also consider pieces that are multi-functional or adaptable, for a longer lifespan – for instance, a cot that can convert to a child's bed.

Beware of cheap brands with no credible ethical certifications, which also almost certainly won't last long. Consider whether the item could be mended or reused in a different way – products made of multiple materials can be hard to recycle and even harder to repair. Be sceptical of "recyclable" labels – recycling the material may be possible in theory, but in practice it can be impossible to find the facilities to do it. If buying synthetic materials, be aware that some give off harmful VOCs (see p.122).

Choose long-lasting items, use them for as long as you can, and, eventually, give them to someone else.

Choosing sustainable materials

Several common furniture materials, as well as some more unusual, greener options, are compared here. If you find a material not listed below, research online or speak to the manufacturer.

FURNISHING MATERIALS

Wood

Ash, beech, oak, and pine are popular woods for furniture and fittings, but all four have been over-logged in Europe and Russia. They often come from ancient forests that need better protection. Douglas fir and cedar tend to come from ancient forests in the US, Canada, or Brazil, and their illegal logging puts delicate ecosystems of birds, fish, and other wildlife at risk.

Before buying any type of wood, check that is has FSC certification or that the wood used was reclaimed.

MDF

While it's cheap and can be made of waste or scrap wood, the binder used is often urea-formaldehyde, which is carcinogenic. As there are few recycling facilities for MDF, it usually ends up in landfill, leaching toxins into the ground.

Bamboo

Quick-growing, versatile, and a lot stronger than it looks, bamboo is often the greenest option for furniture. Make sure it's been sourced sustainably – it can be FSC certified (see p.169), but not many bamboo forests are, as it is technically a grass, not a wood.

Metal

Steel or aluminium is a good bet, as a high percentage of these metals can be recycled.

Recycled plastic

Plastic can be made into pellets and planks that look like wood, which is ideal for outdoor or street furniture. Only buy items made from recycled plastic, so you're not creating more plastic waste.

Cardboard

Corrugated cardboard – perhaps surprisingly – is great for items like chairs and bed frames. It's lightweight, adaptable, and can be moved easily and recycled quickly. Buy online or make your own.

What should I buy to be green when decorating?

Whether you're touching up the skirting boards or installing a new kitchen, there are plenty of better choices you can make to protect the environment.

For greener decorating projects, always see if you can recycle or give away anything you're ripping out or replacing. Use hand tools rather than electric ones, and buy DIY materials in packets or tins rather than plastic, in bulk where possible.

When it comes to choosing paint, avoid those with high levels of volatile organic compounds (VOCs). These chemicals evaporate easily, becoming toxic gases. Many are carcinogenic and cause a range of other health problems when inhaled. Until a few years ago, VOCs were common in all household paints, but most matt and satin paints now contain much lower levels. Look for "breathable" options made of natural materials such as chalk, vegetable dyes, minerals, and china clay. Avoid paint containing vinyl, oils, or petrochemical solvents, which are unsustainable and potentially harmful to animals and humans. Look for paint companies that manufacture in your home country, that don't test on animals, and that have a responsible waste policy.

Most wallpaper isn't particularly eco-friendly. It is often coated in vinyl to make it last longer, so can't be recycled due to its complex make-up, and doesn't biodegrade. Look for recyclable wallpapers that don't contain plastics, are made with paper from sustainable forests, and are printed using non-toxic, water-based inks. Choose wallpaper paste that doesn't contain animal derivatives or toxic solvents.

For wooden kitchen units or floors, always buy recycled or sustainably sourced wood. Alternatively, consider innovative materials such as flooring underlay made of recycled plastic bottles, and kitchen counters formed from plastic taken from the sea and melted down to look like hard wax. These greener options can be expensive, but prices are falling all the time, as demand increases.

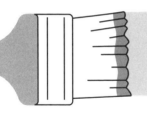

ONE **LITRE OF PAINT** CAN GENERATE
30 LITRES OF **TOXIC WASTE** DURING ITS PRODUCTION

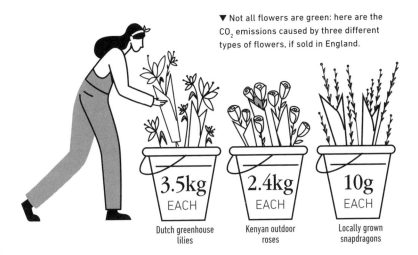

▼ Not all flowers are green: here are the CO_2 emissions caused by three different types of flowers, if sold in England.

3.5kg EACH
Dutch greenhouse lilies

2.4kg EACH
Kenyan outdoor roses

10g EACH
Locally grown snapdragons

Is it okay to buy cut flowers?

The cut-flower industry is a huge source of emissions, with flowers flying thousands of miles to reach your local florist.

The majority of the world's cut flowers are grown in just three countries: Kenya, Ecuador, and Colombia. In fact, 80% of all flowers bought in both the UK and US are imported.

To meet year-round demand, flowers are grown out of season using large amounts of artificial light and heat. They are treated with pesticides, growth regulators, and other chemicals, which harm soil and wildlife, and can cause eutrophication when they enter bodies of water.

After cutting, flowers are wrapped in protective plastic, then kept cool as they are flown and driven to retailers worldwide. The environmental cost is considerable – for instance, the 100 million roses bought each year in the US for Valentine's Day produce 9,000 tonnes of CO_2. To enjoy flowers in a greener way:

- **Buy locally grown** flowers if you can. For blooms grown overseas, the "Fairtrade" mark denotes growers who treat the environment and workers more responsibly.
- **Use a sustainably focused** local florist, rather than an international or online chain.
- **Ask for plastic-free** wrapping and avoid arrangements made with unsustainable plastic florists' foam.
- **As an alternative**, consider a seasonal pot plant, which will last longer than a bouquet.

"Don't throw everything out and start again – *make what you have last.*"

Should I invest in reusable items such as a lunchbox and water bottle?

Reusable food and drink accessories are increasingly popular, but when it comes to everyday items, the most sustainable option is something you already own.

The backlash against single-use plastic is fuelled by the best motives, but we need to make sure we don't use it as an excuse to buy even more stuff. Rather than running out and replacing everything we've got with a more "sustainable" alternative, the greenest way to live is to reduce the number of things we buy, and to use what we already have for as long as we can. For instance, resist the urge to buy a posh "zero-waste" lunchbox if you've already got serviceable plastic food containers at home.

Reusable water bottles are a great way to reduce single-use plastic, but avoid cheap stainless steel or reusable plastic bottles, manufactured in factories thousands of miles away. Choose something you're going to love using – you'll look after it better and will be more likely to take it everywhere you go – made by a company with a clear environmental philanthropic model. For instance, profits from your bottle could be helping to fund clean-water projects.

Plastic straws have become a social no-no. Although plastic is often the most suitable material for people with disabilities because it is more robust, most of us can choose from more eco-friendly alternatives, including steel, bamboo, glass, and even wheat – the original straw! Avoid paper straws as they quickly become soggy and they are not usually recyclable.

Reusable coffee cups are also popular – for more on them, see p.60.

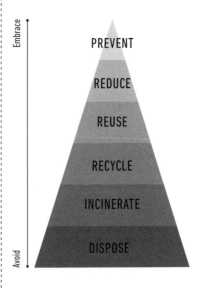

Embrace

Avoid

PREVENT

REDUCE

REUSE

RECYCLE

INCINERATE

DISPOSE

▲ The "waste hierarchy" shows how actions should be prioritized: reusing things you already have is preferable to replacing them.

What's the greenest way to give a present?

Gifting often comes with guilt ("Have I spent enough? Have I spent too much?"), but now there's also eco-anxiety at the sheer amount of stuff we give, receive, and often return to the shops.

While we may love giving and receiving presents, it turns out we're not that sold on the stuff itself – one study in the US, for instance, found that 40% of people surveyed had returned at least one gift to the store after Christmas. So how can we make gifting less wasteful?

A more environmentally conscious approach doesn't mean you have to stop celebrating birthdays, anniversaries, and achievements. If you know someone needs and wants a specific item, by all means

10 million
UNWANTED GIFTS
WERE RECEIVED IN AUSTRALIA IN 2018

buy it as a gift – but if not, consider alternatives that won't deplete the planet's resources, or end up in the bin all too soon.

Birthday fundraisers are an increasingly popular way to mark a special day: the person requests that instead of buying a gift,

friends and family follow a link to donate online to a specific charity or cause.

If the recipient is a child, it's worth checking with parents if they even want their child to receive a gift. Many parents would love to reduce the number of gifts their children receive, but don't know how to express this for fear of causing offence. If it says "no gifts" on a party invitation, respect the request.

To give the gift of a greener life, try these ideas:

- **Swap a physical gift** for a fun experience – such as a day out together, a spa treatment, or a concert.
- **Make your own** home-made gift (edible items are always appreciated), or re-gift an unwanted item you've been given.
- **Plant a tree**, donate to a charity, or adopt an endangered animal in the recipient's name.
- **Put money** in a savings account for a child, instead of buying toys that will soon be discarded.

Are there greener alternatives to wrapping paper?

Whether you view wrapping presents as a chore or a treat, one thing is undeniable: all that giftwrap is anything but a gift for the planet.

Wrapping paper poses real issues for the environment: like all paper, it relies on the use of trees and enormous quantities of water in production – but, crucially, most of it can't be recycled. To check if giftwrap is recyclable, scrunch or rip it: if it doesn't stay scrunched or is hard to rip, then the chances are it's not made purely of paper, so is destined for landfill. Any sticky tape, glitter, plastic ribbon, or other decorative additions stuck to the paper will render it unrecyclable too.

The developed world's appetite for giftwrap is seemingly insatiable, and the energy cost is considerable. For instance, the French buy 20,000 tonnes of paper every Christmas, and in Germany, the amount of energy taken to make all the wrapping paper used annually could power a small town for a year.

Here's how to achieve good-looking gifts while cutting back on the wrap:

- **Use brown paper** or newspaper, both of which are fully recyclable. Don't use sticky tape – use string or ribbon instead, or look for recyclable paper tape with non-plastic adhesive. Swap plastic bows and glitter for natural flourishes such as seasonal foliage sprigs. Kids will love making their own wrapping materials by using home-made vegetable dyes to print designs onto plain paper, or to colour string.
- **Try furoshiki**, the Japanese art of fabric wrapping. Organic cotton wraps can be sourced online, or make your own using squares of scrap material; your gifts will look pretty, and the receiver can reuse the fabric. There are lots of demos online showing how to wrap every shape of gift.
- **Keep and reuse giftwrap**, bags, ribbons, and other bits and pieces of decoration. Wrapping gifts can be an opportunity to be creative with what you've got, rather than buying everything new.

THE UK GETS THROUGH

227,000 MILES OF

WRAPPING PAPER **EVERY CHRISTMAS**

How bad for the environment are greetings cards?

Most of us enjoy sending or receiving a card, but with all that paper, plastic, and emissions adding up, we're sending less-than-good wishes to the planet.

It's estimated that the average card sent by post generates approximately 140g of CO_2 over its lifetime. That might not seem like much, but it all adds up, and you might be surprised by how much those cards contribute to climate change. Globally, we buy and send around seven billion cards a year, which amounts to 980,000 tonnes of carbon released into the atmosphere.

OF THE CARDS BOUGHT **IN THE UK**, ONLY

33% GET RECYCLED

The British send the most cards per person, with over two billion cards bought annually; half of them at Christmas time.

There are several ways in which you can limit your environmental impact and still send your sentiments to your loved ones:

- **Make your own cards** to save the energy needed to make new ones – for bonus green points, use recycled card. The recipient will be even more touched that you made the effort to create something personal to them.
- **If you buy a card**, make sure it comes from a sustainably grown or recycled source (in Europe, look for the FSC logo). Opt for greetings cards without cellophane wrappers – they are actually recyclable but most end up in landfill. Look for cards that have been made by a local artist or designer – thus cutting down on transport emissions; keeping your money in the local economy; and supporting independent businesses, which generally have a lower eco-impact than large companies. Some manufacturers use seed paper, which is studded with flower seeds and can be planted by the recipient, giving the card another purpose beyond the bin. Avoid glitter at all costs – it makes the card unrecyclable.
- **Deliver the card** by hand instead of posting it, if it's local to you, and you don't have to make a special car journey.
- **Consider sending an e-card**, which totally avoids the use of materials and significantly reduces the carbon cost.

Should I buy a real Christmas tree or a plastic one?

For those who celebrate Christmas, this is a familiar dilemma. An artificial tree might save a real one from being chopped down every year, but is it really the more eco-friendly option?

Artificial Christmas trees are made from non-sustainable petroleum-derived plastics, then transported, often over long distances, from factory to retailer. You'd have to use a fake tree for 10 years before it became more energy-efficient than using a real tree each year, but even then you're left, at the end of its life, with a tree that does not decompose. There's no consensus on how long artificial trees take to break down, but they were first produced in the 1920s, and it's likely that most of them are still taking up landfill space. Real trees are the greener option. They're a sustainable resource when farms are appropriately managed and trees are replanted every year. It takes 7 years to grow a 2-metre tree, and throughout that time it's absorbing CO_2. The 100 million Christmas trees growing at any one time in the UK provide an important carbon sink (see p.12).

For a greener Christmas, make sure your tree was grown sustainably and also locally, to reduce the impact of transportation. If you buy a living tree in a pot, you can repot or plant it in the garden after Christmas, extending its life to absorb more carbon. In some areas, you can even rent a potted tree, returning it after Christmas to be replanted.

When disposing of a real tree, take it to a recycling facility that can turn it into compost. Some 7 million trees end up in landfill each year in the UK, where they release methane, a highly potent greenhouse gas, as they break down in the absence of air. If your tree can't be composted, the next best option is to safely burn it.

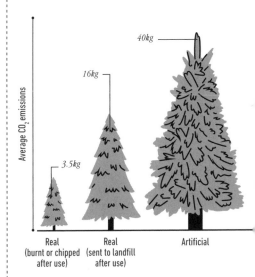

Average CO_2 emissions

3.5kg — Real (burnt or chipped after use)

16kg — Real (sent to landfill after use)

40kg — Artificial

▲ Lifetime carbon emissions – including disposal – show that real trees are greener.

How bad are fireworks for the environment?

Fireworks make any occasion special, but those "Ooh"s and "Ahh"s will turn into "Argh!" and "Oh no!" once you realize how much damage these pretty explosions cause to our planet.

When a firework goes off it releases carbon dioxide and very fine dust particles of metals and other toxins, which pollute the air and are harmful to health. In the US, fireworks give off over 60,000 tonnes of CO_2 a year. In China, spikes in air pollution are often reported around the Chinese New Year, with pollution sometimes reaching dangerous levels.

The substances in fireworks – sulphur, potassium nitrate, and charcoal – pollute not only the air but also the waterways over which they are often exploded, harming aquatic life. The metallic elements, added for colour, seep into soil, building up acidity, which in turn affects the health of plants and animals. And, on top of all that, fireworks are often covered in plastic casing, which, once blown up, remains in the soil and water as microplastics (see p.96).

If you are planning a special celebration, do you really need fireworks? Could you organize a laser show instead? If you want to enjoy fireworks during national celebrations, go to public events rather than having extra fireworks at home.

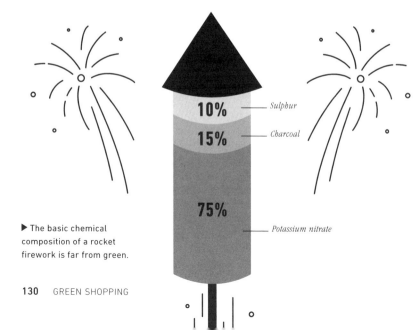

10% —— *Sulphur*

15% —— *Charcoal*

75%

—— *Potassium nitrate*

▶ The basic chemical composition of a rocket firework is far from green.

How can I be green when throwing a party?

Everyone loves a party, but the impact that many decorative items and balloons have on the planet is nothing to celebrate. Luckily, there are enviromentally friendly party alternatives.

Decorations such as streamers and bunting are often made of plastic and designed to be discarded after just one use. Confetti can also be a problem: when it is thrown outside, it's incredibly hard to clean up and often ends up in waterways or littering the ground, posing a risk for animals that might eat it.

Setting off balloons is a lovely way to celebrate an occasion, but have you ever thought about where they land? In the sea, an old balloon can look like a tasty morsel to a turtle or dolphin. On land, small creatures can get entangled in them.

Some balloons are better than others, but all pose problems. Rubber balloons are made with latex tapped from rubber trees. Most of these trees are grown on plantations owned by small-scale farmers. These plantations do benefit our ecosystems – it's estimated that the 16 million trees required by the global balloon industry sequester over 363 million kilograms of carbon from the atmosphere each year. However, even though rubber balloons are technically biodegradable, they take years to decompose once popped, and during that time they litter the seas or land. Chinese lanterns cause a similar issue: the paper takes a long time to biodegrade, and the metal frames can harm animals. They also pose a fire hazard if they are still lit when they land.

Helium balloons are problematic because they are rapidly using up the planet's

---

EATING BALLOON BITS IS
32 TIMES MORE **DEADLY TO BIRDS** THAN INGESTING HARD PLASTIC

---

finite supplies of this inert gas. And mylar (plastic foil) balloons never fully biodegrade.

- **Make your own** streamers and fabric bunting, and reuse them for as long as possible.
- **For confetti**, look for natural versions, such as flower petals; there are also options that dissolve when they come into contact with water, as well as compostable paper confetti that contains seeds. Avoid sequins and glitter (see p.103).
- **Use only rubber latex** balloons, and don't let them fly away.

GREEN
TECHNOLOGY

What's the greenest choice for renewable energy?

Switching from fossil-fuel power to a renewable energy source is one of the easiest green swaps. Understanding how the energy market works will help you make this change.

The consequences of burning fossil fuels such as coal, oil, and gas for power are well documented. These fuels create greenhouse-gas emissions, and come with additional concerns including the impact of fracking on land, and the extra carbon cost – and implications for local resilience – of importing non-renewable energy.

Renewable sources

Wind, solar, hydro, or biomass (made from plant waste or sometimes animal manure) are all renewable forms of energy. Each type has pros and cons. For example, constructing wind turbines or solar panels (which can't be recycled) uses materials and energy. The same is true of hydro dams, which can also lead to deforestation and the displacement of wildlife and people. On the plus side, because these forms of energy are constantly available (or, in the case of biomass, replenishable), the long-term environmental cost of harvesting them is less than that of burning non-renewables.

Pushing for change

Unless you are generating your own power, the electricity that comes to your house isn't from a single source. Instead, electricity from all sources,

renewable or not, goes into a national grid. This may feel frustrating if you want your electricity to be completely green. But the more people switch to green energy tariffs, the greater the pressure on energy suppliers to move away from fossil fuels.

It's encouraging that some countries, including Iceland, Norway, and Kenya, already get almost all of their energy from renewable sources. Elsewhere, Australia's demand for wind and solar

---

RENEWABLE ENERGY SOURCES **OVERTOOK FOSSIL FUELS** IN THE UK FOR THE **FIRST TIME** IN **2019**

---

is growing at 10 times the average rate; in some states, 50% of electricity already comes from wind and solar power. In Germany, renewables including biomass accounted for just under 50% of all energy used in 2019.

Comparison websites, banks, and other companies offer to make the process of changing supplier convenient. Or, you could invest in your own energy source – this involves an initial financial outlay,

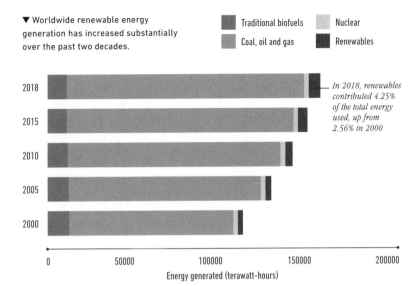

▼ Worldwide renewable energy generation has increased substantially over the past two decades.

Traditional biofuels | Nuclear
Coal, oil and gas | Renewables

In 2018, renewables contributed 4.25% of the total energy used, up from 2.56% in 2000

Energy generated (terawatt-hours)

but can prove very sustainable in the long term. The main options for domestic set-ups are wind and solar.

Here's what to do to move away from fossil fuels:

- **Switch to a green tariff**. Look for a company that uses 100% renewable sources. Energy sources should be clearly stated – if they aren't, ask the supplier to clarify. If you're vegan, you may want to find a supplier who ensures that no animal by-products are used to create biomass gas.
- **If opting for** a company that uses non-renewable sources, check if their values on, say, nuclear energy or fracking align with yours.
- **Around 16 solar panels** will power an average family home. In the US and many other countries,

solar panels can be connected to a national grid, and any excess energy sold back to the energy supplier. Alternatively, energy can be stored off-grid using suitable batteries. Blue-chip companies are working on making solar panels smaller and thinner and increasing the capacity of domestic batteries.

- **Domestic wind turbines** are an option for those with over half a hectare of land. The same options for grid connection or storage apply as for solar panels.
- **Community micro-grids** can power a village or a remote community, usually by wind and/ or solar. These schemes can be efficient and cost-effective when managed well.

What's the greenest way to heat my home?

As far as heating is concerned, being green is about using less energy, finding the most efficient heating system, and swapping to electricity created by renewable resources.

While we might criticize industries such as aviation and fashion for their excessive carbon output, our own homes are a huge source of those same emissions. If we unthinkingly crank up a room's heat by just one degree centigrade, we pump an extra 350kg of carbon dioxide into the atmosphere in a year. Multiply that by millions of homes, and the scale of the issue is clear. The ways in which we can minimize the impact of heating our homes break down into three main areas.

- **Use renewable energy** if you can. Coal and gas, as fossil fuels, are never green – many countries, such as the Netherlands, have banned them in new homes, but replacing the heating system in an existing home is too expensive for many people. If it's an option where you live, consider switching to a green-energy supplier. These companies match the amount of electricity you take from the national supply with the same amount of clean, renewable

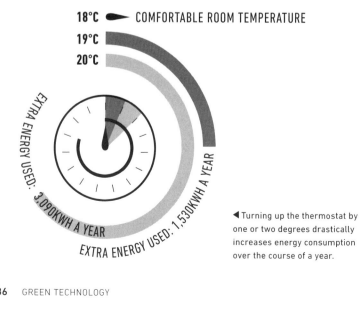

18°C ➡ COMFORTABLE ROOM TEMPERATURE
19°C
20°C

EXTRA ENERGY USED: 3,090KWH A YEAR

EXTRA ENERGY USED: 1,530KWH A YEAR

◀ Turning up the thermostat by one or two degrees drastically increases energy consumption over the course of a year.

energy – so the more users who sign up, the bigger the percentage of renewable energy available in the grid.

- **Heat more efficiently**. Heat pumps are among the most energy-efficient heating methods – they transfer heat from the ground, air, or water outside into your home. They are cheap to run and emissions are low – but they are expensive to install. Modern wood stoves are almost as efficient, but research has found that smoke from them contributes significantly to air pollution. Biomass boilers are essentially high-tech wood stoves. They burn wood pellets, and the resulting ash can be used as compost.

- **Use less energy** for heating. Turning down your heating by just a single degree can save a surprising amount of energy over time. Think about heating only the rooms you are using – turn down the radiators in others. Remote-control systems help you to be more proactive in controlling the temperature of each room, and can reduce usage by up to 5%. Insulation is a must. This means more than double-glazed windows: the areas between floors, walls, and ceilings, as well as your roof space, can almost certainly be insulated better. You can even buy insulating paint! Many countries operate schemes to help with the costs of upgrading domestic insulation.

How can I be green and keep my home cool?

There are ways to stay cool without resorting to energy-hungry, carbon-emitting air conditioning.

Air conditioners (AC) pose the same challenges as heating systems, in that they use huge amounts of energy, and it can be hard, depending on where you live, to ensure that the energy comes from renewable sources. What's more, AC systems contain hydrofluorocarbons (HFCs), notorious greenhouse gases that can be over a thousand times more potent than CO_2 (see p.12), posing a huge threat to the climate.

To keep cool without turning on the AC, create a through-draught by opening windows at opposite sides of a room or building in the early morning, before it gets hot. Then, as the day warms up, keep windows shut and curtains drawn to keep the hot air out. Ensure that your roof, windows, and doors are well insulated to stop cooler air escaping. A ceiling fan can be effective – run it at a low speed, and anticlockwise so that the angled blades create a cooling downdraught. If you have sufficient space outdoors, plant trees or shrubs, or fix awnings to your building to throw shade onto the side of your home that faces the sun.

Is it really worth turning electronic devices off at the wall at night?

Leaving devices on standby overnight might seem convenient, but the environmental impact means we should flick the switch on this habit.

Our devices use up to 90% of their power when on standby. Three-quarters of us leave devices on standby at night, from televisions and dishwashers to game consoles, smart speakers, and phone chargers. Standby mode is thought to be responsible for 1% of global CO_2 emissions.

In the UK, this wasteful habit equates to two power stations' worth of electricity each year. Generally, the older an appliance is, the more energy it eats up in standby mode.

Avoiding standby is one of the easiest ways to cut down the amount of energy you use.

- **Get into the habit** of turning off devices at the plug when not in use. It costs no more to turn them off properly and then on again, and nor does it use up more energy.
- **Invest in energy-saving** (or standby-saving) "smart" plugs (see opposite), which can be turned off and on remotely.

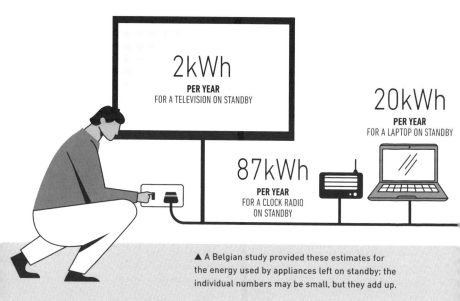

2kWh
PER YEAR
FOR A TELEVISION ON STANDBY

20kWh
PER YEAR
FOR A LAPTOP ON STANDBY

87kWh
PER YEAR
FOR A CLOCK RADIO
ON STANDBY

▲ A Belgian study provided these estimates for the energy used by appliances left on standby; the individual numbers may be small, but they add up.

Will smart technology help my home be more energy-efficient?

"Smart" home technology can help you to manage your money and energy consumption more efficiently, but is not without sustainability issues.

Internet-controlled devices in the home – from smart meters to smart appliances and plugs – can help our households and other buildings to be less wasteful. This "internet of things" enables us to regulate the temperature, turn off appliances when we're out, and reduce our overall energy usage via smart and voice-activated controls. However, introducing this technology into your home can have drawbacks.

Hidden costs

The energy and materials used to manufacture smart electronic devices is reflected in their own carbon footprint.

In addition, as the internet of things grows, so too will the number of appliances that need to remain on standby (see opposite) to communicate with each other, such as voice-activated speakers that offer virtual assistance. The carbon emissions generated from keeping our smart electronics on standby mode are expected to rise by 20% in the next five years.

Aside from energy consumption, high-tech appliances often need updating or replacing more regularly, as new technology comes in that is incompatible with older gadgets.

So, think about your needs before you invest in smart tech.

- **If your aim** is to buy less or "make do and mend" when it comes to appliances and electronics, smart technology is not the way to go.

SMART TECH COULD REDUCE THE AVERAGE OFFICE BUILDING'S ENERGY USE BY **20%**

- **If you do want to use** smart tech, try to stick to devices that improve home energy-efficiency. A smart meter for your electricity or gas shows you exactly how much energy you use, when, and how much it costs, which helps you to be mindful about your consumption. Smart plugs can also save energy: they can turn off several devices in one go and operate appliances on a timer; plus, you can activate them via an app wherever you are. These types of technology can be highly effective at saving energy in offices, too.

What's the most eco-friendly type of battery?

The multitude of battery-hungry devices in our lives means it's vital to be mindful of how we use and dispose of these potentially toxic items.

In 2018, approximately 191,000 tonnes of batteries were sold in the EU. Batteries contain heavy metals, many of which are mined in corrupt conflict zones such as Afghanistan, where workers often endure miserable conditions. The mining has an impact on land as well as on the indigenous communities, who are often displaced.

If batteries are disposed of in landfill they leach toxic chemicals into the soil, potentially contaminating groundwater. Decaying batteries also release greenhouse gases.

Battery innovations for renewable-energy capabilities are fuelling huge leaps forward, as are improvements in the range and reliability of electric cars. For domestic usage, though, batteries haven't evolved much in terms of efficiency, and advice on which are the most environmentally friendly is scant. You can minimize the impact of your battery use in several ways:

- **Reduce your overall need** for batteries. Consider alternatives such as solar phone chargers or wind-up dynamo torches.
- **Always recycle batteries**. You can find recycling bins in many stores as well as recycling centres.
- **Avoid buying single-charge** batteries. Rechargeable batteries last for up to 1,000 charges. There are greener options when choosing rechargeable batteries, too. Look for nickel metal hydride (NiMH) batteries, which hold their charge for longer than other rechargeables. Combine these with a smart charger, which shuts off when the battery is fully charged.

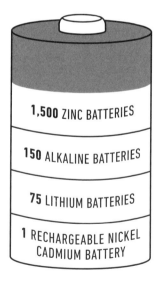

1,500 ZINC BATTERIES

150 ALKALINE BATTERIES

75 LITHIUM BATTERIES

1 RECHARGEABLE NICKEL CADMIUM BATTERY

▲ Each type of battery has a different lifespan: the above quantities will all provide the same amount of energy.

Are some laptops and tablets greener than others?

In many ways, technology helps us to be more sustainable, but the hardware on which it relies on is often the opposite of green. Being informed can help you make eco-conscious choices.

It's estimated that in 2019 there were approximately 2 billion computers (including laptops) and 1 billion tablets in the world. All those devices cause an enormous amount of e-waste – electrical or electronic waste. In the first quarter of 2019, for instance, over 122,000 tonnes of e-waste was generated in the UK, and much of it ended up in landfill.

Aside from the waste issue, materials such as polyvinyl chloride (PVC) are commonly used in the manufacture of computers and tablets. These can emit harmful chemicals during the production process, and again if a device is incinerated after use.

There are also questions over the ethical credentials of many seemingly forward-thinking tech brands. In some companies, the use of child labour has been exposed, and, as with batteries and phones, components are often mined in conflict zones. As tempting as it is to update or replace your tech, the green approach is to buy less and make it last. Consider the following before you invest:

- **Buy reconditioned** or recycled rather than brand new, to decrease the demand for new raw materials.
- **Favour desktop computers** over laptops, as they are easier to repair and upgrade. For the same reason, choose laptops over tablets.
- **If you do choose** to buy a new product, identify which brands have clear policies with regard to human rights, fair wages, and working conditions, and check their policies regarding "conflict" minerals. A good starting point

THE **AVERAGE LAPTOP** REQUIRES **10** TIMES ITS WEIGHT IN **POLLUTANT CHEMICALS** TO PRODUCE

is to check whether a brand is "TCO Certified" – an international standard that identifies computers, tablets, and phone brands with a responsible and sustainable supply chain.

- **Ideally, try to establish** whether any toxic chemicals have been used in the manufacturing process. A growing number of companies are working towards eliminating such harmful substances from their products.

How can I limit electrical waste?

Our "throw away and upgrade" consumerist culture is resulting in unsustainable levels of e-waste. It's time to rethink our approach to electrical technology.

Frequent updates and tech trends mean that electronic devices and electrical appliances are rarely designed to last. As consumers, we are encouraged to discard older models on a frequent basis, and to reject any item with a minor defect – whether it's a toaster with a jammed button or a phone with a cracked screen. In recent years, our consumption of household electrical appliances has shot up: in 2018, UK households spent 11 billion pounds on appliances – a billion more than in the previous year. This "planned obsolescence" has a huge

---

EACH YEAR THE WORLD PRODUCES AN ESTIMATED

50 MILLION TONNES OF E-WASTE

---

eco-impact, adding to a growing mountain of toxic e-waste, of which only around 20% is actually recycled.

Recycling is clearly key in tackling the global e-waste issue. But we can also review our whole approach to how we purchase and maintain our appliances and gadgets. Remembering the mantra of "reduce, reuse, recycle" can help change our mindset.

- **Reduce**. There are steps you can take at the start of the purchasing cycle. If you can, spend a bit more on a higher-quality product. Items that can either be mended easily (often those from independent or smaller brands) or that are built to last longer – ideally a lifetime – mean you throw less away, reducing your waste in the long term.
- **Reuse**. You may think that mending products is outside your skill set. However, growing numbers of "repair cafés" are popping up. These informal events aim to teach people basic skills so they can do their own repairs, whether that's rewiring a plug or replacing individual parts of a computer.
- **Recycle**. Many countries, the US and the UK included, have nationwide schemes where you can take electricals to be recycled. Toasters, drills, hairdryers, TVs, and more don't need to be tossed into landfill. Once you've taken them to your local drop-off point, the items can be collected and dismantled safely. Computers, laptops, and tablets can also be dropped off at specialist recycling centres, though remember to clear the hard drive or local storage of personal data first.

Is my smartphone killing the planet?

It's estimated that there are now more smartphones than people on the planet. The manufacture and disposal of our phones are both clear environmental concerns.

The US alone has more than a quarter of a billion phones ready to be recycled, and an additional 11 million are added to this figure every month. It's estimated that less than 20% of these phones end up actually being recycled.

The metals that are used in the production of smartphones are precious resources. Valuable metals such as tungsten are often mined in extremely poor working conditions, sometimes in conflict zones.

If phones aren't recycled, more and more of these metals need to be mined to keep up with the demand for new models. And when phones end up in landfill, toxic elements such as mercury and lead leach into the soil, contaminating groundwater.

To reduce the enormous impact of this problem we need to think more carefully about our phones' lifecycles:

- **Don't take an** automatic upgrade unless you really need it.
- **Recycle your old phone** via a trustworthy company. When a phone is properly recycled, metals such as gold, platinum, and copper are recovered. This is vastly preferable to simply dumping your phone. There are charities and initiatives for recycling phones, and some brands will take back old handsets free of charge and recycle the phones in properly monitored facilities.
- **When changing your phone**, opt for a reconditioned secondhand phone or seek out independent suppliers that operate a fair mining policy and supply chain in the manufacture of their smartphones.

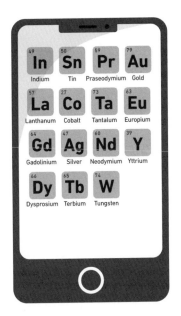

▲ Mining "rare-earth metals", as well as the other precious metals in most smartphones, has serious environmental effects.

GREEN
GARDEN

How can I make my garden as green as it can be?

Not all gardens are green. There are a few things you can do when planning, or modifying, your garden to make it work harder for the wildlife and environment around you.

A garden can be a haven from the busy world, a source of food and flowers, and a space to reconnect with nature – or it can be a drain on resources and a burden on soil.

When soil is covered over with slabs or concrete it can't soak up rainwater or take in carbon via plants. Plants are crucial to soil health, supplying carbon to nourish soil fauna and ensure soil structure, and maintaining the nutrient cycle. Bare soil becomes eroded and depleted. It might not be something you give much thought to,

but soil, when properly looked after, supports a rich biodiversity and acts as a carbon sink (see p.208).

Choosing plants

Growing plants that aren't native to your area can be a problem. Plants that don't naturally flourish in dry climates, for instance, will need a lot of watering to remain healthy if planted in an area with low rainfall.

Eco-friendly gardens work best when your choice of landscaping and/or plants matches the terrain

▼ There are plenty of low-effort, low-cost ways to make your garden green (in every sense).

GROW **NATIVE** TREES AND PLANTS

COVER THE SOIL **WITH PLANTS**, NOT CONCRETE

and climate you're in. A "green" garden in California is going to look very different from one in Germany.

Battling climate change

With some clever design, your garden can actually help you mitigate some of the effects of climate change or extreme weather events in your local environment. Trees provide shade, so if they are close to your home they can reduce your need for air conditioning in hot weather (see p.137). Planting tall shrubs near your house or putting up a trellis for climbing plants will have the same effect, cooling the air outside your walls.

Your garden can act as a storm drain and help keep the land around your house from flooding. A "rain garden" is a grouping of plants in a low-lying area of ground that slows the run-off

of heavy downfalls. Green roofs can also help soak up excess rainwater. Capturing, managing, and conserving water is key to an eco-friendly garden, so make this a cornerstone of your design and planting.

IN **CITIES**, AN ESTIMATED

22–36% OF THE LAND

AREA IS **TAKEN UP BY GARDENS**

A wildlife habitat

A green outdoor space can provide a refuge for insects, birds, and other wildlife, most of which have experienced habitat loss over the last hundred years. Since the 1940s, the UK has lost 97% of its "unimproved" grassland (land that isn't being used for agriculture or gardens), causing the destruction of many species' natural homes. We need to create spaces for our wildlife again, and "rewilding" our gardens is the perfect way to start.

Every garden has plenty of green potential that you can unlock:

- **Plant a diverse** range of location-appropriate plants to attract insects, which in turn will provide food for birds and other wildlife.
- **Avoid paving over your garden** or putting down artifical grass.
- **Start a compost heap** – an essential for a green garden; see p.160 for more.

MAKE YOUR GREEN SPACE A BUG PARADISE

Which insects should I be attracting to my garden?

We need more insects – everywhere. Making whatever space you have more welcoming to bugs is key to supporting biodiversity in your local area.

Insects play a vital role in pollinating crops and other plants. They also provide food for larger animals, and break down organic matter to return nutrients to the soil. However, more than 40% of the world's insect species are dying out. According to one study, Germany lost 76% of its flying insect population between 1989 and 2016. It's time to nurture the survivors.

A quick online search will show you which insects you'll be able to attract where you live. While some

 ACROSS EUROPE, NEARLY **10%** WILD **BEE** SPECIES ARE FACING **EXTINCTION**

aren't welcome if you're growing food, and many are a nuisance when you're outside, there are also lots of beneficial insect species.

- **To invite butterflies and moths**, grow nectar-rich flowers such as buddleia and verbena, long-stemmed flowers or grasses for shelter, and trees such as oak, willow, and birch to provide habitat and breeding spots.

- **To encourage creepy-crawlies** such as beetles and spiders, create dark, shady spaces with rotten logs and undergrowth.

- **Bees like a wide range** of different flowers – some prefer tubular ones, such as foxgloves; others flat, open ones, such as ox-eye daisies. Plant them in sunny spots, ensuring there is a mix of colours and that their blooming times are varied, so you'll have flowers for as long as possible, providing nectar nearly all year round. Flowering trees such as willow provide masses of forage for bees early in the year.

- **Create a wildflower meadow** to provide habitat and food for insects. You can even plant one in a pot, if you're short on space. For best results, dig out weeds first, ensure the area isn't over-fertilized (wildflowers prefer poor soil), and sow it in the spring or autumn.

- **Avoid pesticides** – they kill welcome as well as unwelcome bugs. The right mix of plants can deter any bugs you don't want. Mosquitos don't like strong-smelling plants, flies have an aversion to basil, and rosemary will keep away cabbage moths.

How can I make my garden a habitat for wildlife?

Your garden might look lovely, but is it a happy home for small creatures? Some small changes can make a big difference to local wildlife such as birds and frogs.

Often the easiest way to encourage wildlife is to stop keeping everything neat and tidy, for example, by letting long grasses grow, or by not over-trimming your hedges (leave the space below them undisturbed too). If you attract insects (see left), then their natural predators, such as frogs, bats, and birds, will follow.

Take time to research the most effective ways of attracting the range of wildlife particular to your local area. If you live in a city or suburban area, make sure you've got holes in your garden fences, so that wildlife such as hedgehogs can move between gardens to find food and water.

CREATING A WELCOMING SPACE FOR WILDLIFE

Shelter

Plant trees, leafy shrubs, and tall grasses for cover, and help small creatures by creating refuge among undergrowth or in wood piles. Create a bug hotel out of strips of bark, straw, moss, logs, pine cones, or tubes of cardboard.

Food

Help your neighbourhood birds by putting up feeders that predators such as cats can't get to. Growing sunflowers is another great way to feed your bird friends.

Water

Provide a small, shallow pool with rocks, twigs, or other helpful things to perch on, and a ramp so small creatures can climb out. Bees, for instance, love a pool of water to drink from.

Nest space

Install bird boxes in suitable locations around your garden; for instance, in Europe, most birds prefer a bird box that faces north-east (away from direct sun and prevailing winds). Make sure that cats can't get to the boxes easily.

Is it okay to have a lawn?

Lawns look neat and are nice for kids to play on, but they aren't particularly useful for our surrounding environment – and in some cases, they could be damaging it.

Lawns are an improvement on tarmac or concrete, but otherwise they don't do much except look pretty – and, to be green, that's not enough.

First things first: for those who live anywhere where a lawn wouldn't easily grow, then it's definitely not a green option. Overriding your natural environment requires constant, intensive intervention, often to the detriment of native plants and wildlife.

Irrigating a lawn is a problem in countries prone to droughts, as lawns are incredibly thirsty. Also, replacing native plants with grass can reduce the ability of the ground to soak up sudden heavy downpours, because the soil under a lawn is often more compacted than in plant beds.

While lawns do play their part in the carbon cycle (see p.208), they don't sequester as much carbon dioxide as trees or other plants. What's more, lawns are often sprayed with chemicals, which then leach into soil and waterways, damaging ecosystems and contributing to eutrophication.

If you really want a lawn, there are ways you can help make it greener and more multipurpose without harming the environment. Ultimately,

▼ The ability of different types of plant life to absorb carbon from the air varies – an unkempt meadow is more effective than a lawn.

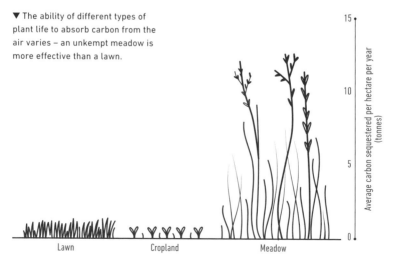

Average carbon sequestered per hectare per year (tonnes)

15

10

5

0

Lawn   Cropland   Meadow

we should be working with nature, encouraging it and helping it grow, not buzzcutting it into submission once a fortnight. It's time to look at your lawn and see what else it can do.

- **Swap a manicured lawn** for a clover, wildflower, or native-grass meadow. Cutting the grass far less frequently will encourage native flowers to seed. Try holding off mowing to just twice, or even once, a year, which gives flowers a chance to complete their life cycle and reseed.

TURF LAWNS COVER OVER

16 million
HECTARES OF LAND IN THE US

- **When you do cut the lawn**, let the grass grow longer between cuts and recycle the clippings by leaving them to decompose on the lawn. This feeds the soil, helping to increase the amount of CO_2 that the lawn can absorb.
- **Create your own allotment** by converting a section of your lawn into a vegetable garden.
- **Stop using pesticides** or other harmful chemicals.
- **Make sure you're catching** and collecting any excess rainwater to use on your lawn (see p.153).

How polluting are lawnmowers?

There's no need to go as far as cutting the grass with hand shears, but some lawnmowers are better than others.

If you do need to mow your lawn, avoid a petrol-powered mower. The fuel is unsustainable, and this type of mower releases noxious and polluting gases, including carbon monoxide and nitrogen oxides. One study concluded that lawnmowers give out 11 times as much air pollution, hour for hour of use, as an average new petrol car.

That leaves you with either an old-fashioned push mower or an electric one. With zero emissions (and a decent workout), a push mower works out the greenest option. If you go for an electric mower, make sure you're on a renewable tariff.

If you are mowing the lawn to improve its condition and even out patchy regrowth, you can also try planting micro-clover. This can help to even out growth by feeding nitrogen down to the roots of the grass. Another option is to use a fine rake to scratch out all the dead roots, for less irregular regrowth.

"A garden can become a microcosm of *eco-friendly practices.*"

What's the greenest way to water the garden?

Fresh water is an increasingly precious resource. A green gardener keeps water usage down, by irrigating cleverly and reusing as much water as possible.

The most water-efficient garden is one that is filled with native plants. These will be accustomed to the rainfall levels you usually get in your local area, so will need less watering than plants that hail from other climates.

Some local authorities prohibit watering lawns and gardens. Even if restrictions aren't in place, be smart with your water. Sprinklers and hoses waste water – sprinklers are often left on for too long, and hoses water indiscriminately unless used with a trigger control. As well as wasting water, overwatering can impact on the health of plants, if they become waterlogged.

- **Make sure your soil** is healthy with compost or mulch – it will retain moisture for longer, so you'll have to water it less often.
- **Water plants early** in the day or at dusk, so less of the water evaporates before soaking into the soil.
- **Water your plants** right on the roots, to avoid wasted run-off.
- **Reuse your bath** or washing-up water (known as grey water) on your plants (provided you're not using too many artificial cleansers or chemicals).

- **Use a drip-irrigation system** if you've got a large space or plants on a wall, to direct water exactly where it's needed.
- **Invest in a lidded rain barrel** to capture rainfall and water from the roof, and use this on your garden instead of tap water. If you have space, consider installing a domestic rainwater-harvesting system with an underground tank, to store heavy rainfalls.

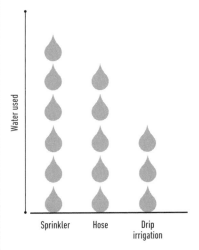

▲ Drip-irrigation methods use less water than a hose and 50% less water than a sprinkler, because water isn't wasted due to evaporation or run-off.

What materials are greenest for garden surfaces?

What you cover the ground with – and whether you cover it at all – makes a big difference to how eco-friendly your garden is. Some surfaces can be surprisingly damaging.

For too long we've covered our soil with impermeable materials, such as concrete and tarmac, stripping the ground of the capacity to soak up rain. The fashion for paved driveways and yards in Western urban and suburban housing has caused an increase in flooding in towns and cities, as excess water literally has nowhere to go.

Dense materials, such as stone and concrete, also trap heat during the day then release it at night, creating what's called a "heat island" effect in urban areas. The increased heat at night can make it harder for us to sleep.

Concrete in particular is an eco-nightmare: the immense global scale of its production uses so much

---

5.2 million
PROPERTIES IN ENGLAND ARE AT RISK OF **BEING FLOODED**

---

energy that if the cement industry were a country, it would rank third in the world for carbon emissions.

If you want hard landscaping in your garden and still want to be green, think about how whatever you put down will interfere with how the ground beneath it keeps the area habitable – whether that's by absorbing rainwater or regulating temperatures. When weighing up your options, consider where the materials came from, how long they will last, whether they can be recycled, and whether your surfacing can be maintained without the use of toxic chemicals that can harm wildlife, impacting on local ecosystems.

- **Choose porous materials** such as decking or gravel, that will let surface water soak through. Stone paving with gaps filled with sand rather than cement is another solution to the drainage issue.

- **Avoid covering** your entire garden. Having more plants in front gardens and on the street helps regulate summer temperatures to avoid the heat-island effect. A leafy garden can also act as a protective barrier between your house and the street, filtering pollution and dust from the air.

GARDEN FLOORING MATERIALS

Lawn

A lawn is preferable to covering the ground with materials as it will soak up water and trap carbon – but only to an extent (see p.150 for more).

Astroturf

Avoid; it's made of plastic and does nothing for the soil or wildlife. Although it is porous, rainwater tends to run off the compacted soil beneath it.

Gravel

A good option for hard landscaping: effective at allowing water to drain through, and cheaper than paving slabs.

Concrete

Avoid; in addition to its immense carbon footprint, concrete is impermeable, so can cause drainage problems, increasing the risk of flooding.

Stone paving or bricks

Depending on what the gaps between the stones or bricks are filled with, paving has drainage potential – avoid cement (though weeds will grow).

Plastic paving

While new plastic isn't green, paving slabs made of recycled plastic – with holes to allow for water drainage – can be a good option.

Wooden decking

Only choose if made from sustainably grown or recycled wood. Gaps between the boards allow for drainage, but it often requires toxic stains or sealants.

Plastic decking

Avoid; while plastic decking doesn't need maintenance, it's made of polyvinyl chloride (PVC) and can't be recycled or reused afterwards.

Composite decking

Made from recycled plastic and compressed wood scraps, composite decking is long-lasting and allows for water drainage.

Should I be using my garden to grow food?

The most eco-friendly gardens are those that produce food. Anyone who has a green space – or even a balcony or a few plant pots – can do it.

Many of the environmental problems associated with the production and distribution of food worldwide can be alleviated on a small, personal scale by growing your own. Food grown at home has no air miles (see p.48) or packaging (see p.52). It can also be cultivated organically, without the use of intensive chemical input.

And, since you've put in the hard work and heart into helping it grow, you're less likely to waste it than shop-bought food.

Growing your own food can be especially rewarding if you're moving away from a meat-heavy diet and towards eating more plants; having your own supply will be convenient,

▼ Just 4 square metres of beds can provide a substantial harvest of fruit and veg over a 6 month growing season.

MORE THAN 25KG OF PRODUCE OVER *6 months*

and will also seriously cut down your food bills. Growing fruit and vegetables will also allow you to make your own chutney, jam, pickles, and so on, further reducing your reliance on supermarkets.

Studies have found that growing food in front gardens helps build communities. Seasonal gluts of food encourage us to make friends with neighbours to share the bounty, and create connections with other food-growing people. Supporting local food systems rather than complex global supply chains has a hugely beneficial effect on your environment, reducing emissions, waste, and plastic, and improving soil health.

On top of all these advantages, growing your own food is good for you. It lowers stress levels, promoting a sense of achievement and wellbeing – a little bit of repetitive physical labour can also do wonders for your mental health.

Think of your garden as a gateway into a local growing community. It may be time to make "grow food not lawns" your new mantra.

- **Don't take on** too much at once – if you've never grown anything before, start small, with herbs or one or two of your favourite fruit or veg (there's no point growing rows and rows of a vegetable you don't like).
- **Be realistic**. Don't sow so many seeds that you don't have time to

tend to everything; even a few plants can be very productive.

- **Consult online tutorials**, gardening sites, and books to learn what to plant when for your own supply of fresh vegetables, fruit, and herbs year-round.
- **If you don't have a garden**, don't despair: you can grow food in pots on a balcony (think tomatoes, herbs, or strawberries) or even on kitchen windowsills.
- **Sign up for a local allotment** or, if you aren't keen to take on the sole responsibility for a plot and want to share skills with

---

REPLACING A FIFTH OF BOUGHT FOOD WITH **HOME-GROWN** SAVES
30kg OF CO_2 A YEAR, ON AVERAGE

---

others, get involved in a community garden. Can you enlist a like-minded team of people at work, a friendship group, or a playgroup to get together to plant, tend, and harvest a garden?

- **When buying compost**, avoid peat – formed from partly decomposed plant matter over thousands of years, peatlands are valuable water retainers, diverse habitats, and important carbon sinks.

How does permaculture work?

Don't be put off by the fancy-sounding name – a lot of this is common sense. Embracing the values of permaculture will set you on your way to a sustainable garden.

The term "permaculture" was first used in the 1970s, but the concept is ancient. Permaculture is a farming system based on the principle of using and learning from your environment to help plants grow. It's the opposite of industrial monocrop-planting (see p.41). In permaculture, plants grow in harmony with nature, not against it. With just four crops (soya beans, wheat, rice, and corn) accounting for 50% of all the food grown globally, most industrial agriculture doesn't encourage the diversity promoted by permaculture. The small gene pool of commercial crops also makes them vulnerable to pest and disease can wipe out vast swathes of crops.

As well as diversity, permaculture promotes long-term, rather than just seasonal, sustainability. Maintaining soil health, planting organically, and echoing the patterns found in nature are key. Each element of an ecological system is interconnected. So, try to mimic nature in your garden design, letting it do the work for you. For example:

- **Practice "companion" planting.** Leeks and carrots work well together, as each drives away the other's pests.
- **Allow space for wildflowers** near vegetable patches to attract bees, which pollinate produce, increasing yields.

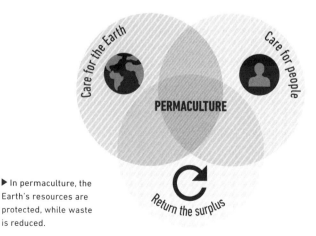

▶ In permaculture, the Earth's resources are protected, while waste is reduced.

How can I reduce plastic in my garden?

If you've tackled plastic waste in your kitchen and bathroom, it's time for your garden to go plastic-free too.

From trowels to plant labels, there are lots of ways plastic can creep into your garden. Plant pots are a horticultural essential, and plastic ones are the cheapest to mass-produce. Most end up either in landfill or being burnt.

THE **PLASTIC PLANT POTS** AND SEED TRAYS UK GARDENERS BUY **EACH YEAR** TOTAL, ON AVERAGE,

500 million

Not all plastic in the garden is environmentally unhelpful. Polytunnels extend the growing season and make it possible to grow a wider range of produce and flowers at home. Having a small one in your garden can reduce your carbon footprint, enabling you to grow your own fruit and vegetables more easily. At the end of its life, the plastic can be recycled into lower-grade items such as refuse sacks.

For the plastic that's really not worth it, it's not difficult to find alternatives.

- **Opt for metal** or wooden versions of gardening tools and supplies, if you need to buy new ones.
- **Look for biodegradable** pots, which can be planted straight into the ground, made from materials such as rice husk and bamboo. Or you could make your own from newspaper, which can be folded to create a pot.
- **Reuse containers** made of natural materials such as wood or clay, or anything you can repurpose (baths, wellies, metal canisters – even an old pair of jeans can become a wall-hanging planter), rather than buying plastic.
- **Make use of plastic waste** from the kitchen. Give empty yogurt pots, milk containers, or drinks bottles a new life by reusing them to grow seedlings.
- **Look for recycling** or sharing schemes in garden centres for plant pots and seed trays.
- **If you're in** a gardening community, can you share or rent larger items rather than buying new or using once?

Is a compost heap always a good idea?

If you've got the space, a compost heap or bin will give you back nutritionally rich soil that will help your garden blossom and food grow.

Turning food waste into compost addresses two environmental issues. First, it keeps rotting food out of landfill, where it would give off the greenhouse gas methane. And secondly, it nourishes and replenishes your garden soil, enabling you to grow your own food, or create a healthy natural environment for wildlife (see p.156 and p.149).

Composting is a simple process, in which organic matter such as food or garden cuttings is digested by microbes and worms, turning it into

---

A COMPOST HEAP CAN RECYCLE
150kg OF FOOD WASTE A YEAR

---

a carbon-rich mulch. To make your own compost, you'll need a container, or a dedicated place in the garden to start a heap. Buy a plastic compost bin or, for a greener solution, make your own container using surplus wood. Add a mixture of nitrogen-rich "green" waste, such as grass clippings and fruit and veg peelings, and carbon-rich "brown" waste, which can be dry twigs, cuttings, or even cardboard. Add the green and the brown in alternating layers; keeping a balance between the two will provide microbes with everything they need to break waste down.

Your compost heap or bin should be moist but not too wet, with air circulating through it, and it should be able to drain. A lid will keep in moisture and warmth, helping waste break down more quickly. Putting it in the sunshine will speed things up, too. You will need to "turn", or mix up, your compost from time to time to keep it aerated. It should be ready to spread on the garden after about 6 months. It will be dark brown, almost black, and crumbly.

- **Know what can be** put into your compost: crushed eggshells, egg boxes, and plastic-free teabags are all in, but meat and dairy are out, as they can smell and attract rats. Avoid composting weeds after they have flowered – most home compost heaps aren't hot enough to destroy their seeds, so you risk unwittingly spreading them around your garden with the compost.
- **If you don't** have space for your own, there are community compost programmes that you can join.

Is it worth getting a wormery?

No room for a compost heap? Don't despair – this is your alternative: an ingenious way to deal with your kitchen waste at home.

If you want to recycle your own food waste but have limited space, a wormery could be the perfect solution. Worms will efficiently process food scraps, turning them into compost and liquid fertilizer for houseplants or window boxes. You can buy a ready-made wormery, complete with worms, or make one yourself; look online for retailers or DIY projects. The worms should be red worms (also known as tiger worms or brandling worms) rather than common earthworms.

A simple wormery has two sections. The worms live in the upper part,

into which you put food waste between layers of sawdust or damp shredded newspaper. Beneath that is a sump where liquid collects. The upper chamber should take up around two-thirds of the total space, and can be divided with a series of stacking trays.

Most kitchen waste can go into your wormery, but don't feed your worms meat, fish, bones, or dairy products, or anything spicy, salty, or vinegary. Wormeries should be kept at 10–30°C – a shed or sheltered balcony are good locations.

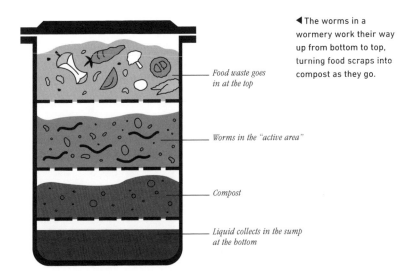

◀ The worms in a wormery work their way up from bottom to top, turning food scraps into compost as they go.

Food waste goes in at the top

Worms in the "active area"

Compost

Liquid collects in the sump at the bottom

Which houseplants are best for cleaning the air?

Indoor greenery does more than just look pretty in a corner or on a shelf – it's good for you and the environment. Viva the houseplant revolution!

Houseplants enhance your immediate environment by taking in carbon dioxide, releasing oxygen, and filtering pollutants and VOCs (see p.122) from the air. Studies show that having more plants inside your home also helps lower stress and promotes calm.

NASA, the US space agency, famously demonstrated the air-filtering properties of houseplants in the 1980s, by measuring the quantities of various substances in a chamber with a plant over time. It is worth noting that the conditions of the study did not resemble real-life living or working environments, so the results should be taken with a pinch of salt. Be that as it may, having plants inside your home is only ever going to improve the air quality, which is ideal if you're in the middle of a big city.

▼ Studies have shown that many common houseplants absorb the harmful substances shown below from the air.

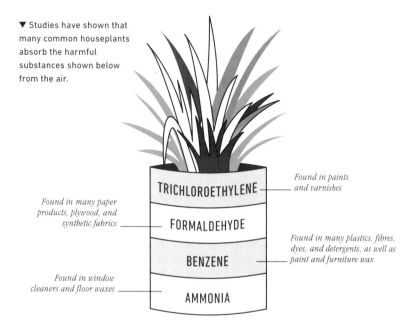

TRICHLOROETHYLENE — *Found in paints and varnishes*

Found in many paper products, plywood, and synthetic fabrics — FORMALDEHYDE

BENZENE — *Found in many plastics, fibres, dyes, and detergents, as well as paint and furniture wax*

Found in window cleaners and floor waxes — AMMONIA

Some of the most effective plants are widely available and inexpensive. Here's where to start if you want to add some greenery to your home:

- **One of the best** species for filtering out toxins such as benzene and formaldehyde is a peace lily (*Spathiphyllum wallisii*). English ivy (*Hedera helix*) is another one of the best air purifiers. Grow it in baskets hung from the ceiling, or in a small pot. Broadleaf lady palms (*Rhapis excelsa*) and dragon trees (*Dracaena marginata*), while slow growers, are effective year in, year out at removing toxins from the air.
- **If you want** something that will grow quickly, opt for a or spider plant (*Chlorophytum comosum*).
- **For those who** don't have green fingers, hard-to-kill devil's ivy (*Epipremnum aureum*) is ideal.

A UK SURVEY FOUND THAT **80%** OF **16–24 YEAR OLDS** OWN AT LEAST ONE **HOUSEPLANT**

- **It's not just plants** that can help the air quality at home. Certain cut flowers, such as chrysanthemums and Barberton daisies, also act as efficient natural filters.
- **Whenever possible**, choose plants or cut flowers that have been grown organically and locally, to avoid unnecessary pollution and air miles.

Does it matter where my plants have come from?

Being aware of the provenance of your plants can help you choose the greenest ones.

Plants and seeds have a supply chain that you can trace – and, as with any other industry, there are multiple opportunities for excess carbon emissions along that supply chain. In the plant industry, the two most carbon-heavy practices are forced growing under lights and heat, and international shipping. It's worth bearing in mind that the greenhouse-gas output of the former can outweigh that of the latter.

When buying plants, ask the garden centre or shop where their plants come from. Opt for those grown locally if you can, and choose native plants where possible, as they will have required less energy-heavy intervention to grow.

If you're growing from seed, it's a little easier – buy from organic seed catalogues. Or, alternatively, seek out seed-exchange schemes, so you can swap seeds with other gardeners, either in person or through the post.

WORK
AND PLAY

FOR EVERY 100 PEOPLE WHO **WORK FROM HOME TWICE A WEEK**, AN ESTIMATED **63.5** TONNES OF CO_2 EMISSIONS ARE AVOIDED ANNUALLY

Where's the greenest place to work?

Millions of us have now experienced working from home, but there are pros and cons to each workplace setup.

A traditional office's green credentials depend on how eco-friendly the company is; not all offices proactively implement green measures. A daily commute can have a significant carbon footprint too, particularly if you drive.

Co-working spaces use less floor area per person than a traditional office, so needs less heating. You may also be able to choose a local space to keep your journey low-carbon. However, you're unlikely to have a say in how the building is run: many modern co-working spaces have energy-hungry features such as excessive neon lighting and in-office bars.

Working from home has the obvious advantage of cutting out travel. During 2020's lockdown, 18 million people in the UK switched to home working, which reduced air pollution by up to 50% in some urban spots, and cut energy-related emissions by 17%. In addition, you're in charge of the energy tariff, so can switch to renewable sources to power lights, heating, and equipment. You may miss out on some green office systems, though, such as electronic-waste recycling (see p.142).

Ultimately, the greenest place to work depends on your situation:

- **Walk or cycle** to the office if you can, and encourage your company to be more green (see opposite).
- **If you drive** to work, consider if you could work from home instead.

How can I make my workplace greener?

From company-wide initiatives to simple green swaps, there are plenty of ways to cut back on waste and carbon emissions in the office.

In addition to managing the recycling of waste, some of the greenest steps offices can take are to ensure that their heating, air-conditioning systems, and lighting are efficient – with systems and lighting on timers, or responsive to when people are using a particular space – and that a building is well (and safely) insulated. Companies can also invest in efficient electronics, swap to a renewable energy tariff, and, if manufacturing products, look into offsetting their carbon emissions. Signing up to an energy-emissions audit is a great way for companies to understand where they can improve.

Workspaces tend to be greener when employees feel included and responsible. If an environmental team isn't already in place, you could suggest instigating one.

Running an audit of where you are now and finding a strategy for where you want to get to is key to measuring success. There are plenty of ways to build environmental strategies into your office's everyday decision-making:

- **Look at how many** plastic stationery items you have and see where substitutes can be made: for example, ordering wooden pencils instead of pens. Avoid providing pens, notepads, and branded merchandise for board meetings and company conferences.
- **If your office** hasn't already done so, swap to LED light bulbs. They are more energy-efficient than compact fluorescent lamps (CFLs), although CFLs are also far better than traditional incandescent bulbs.
- **Avoid printing** unless absolutely necessary; print double-sided, avoid colour printing, and recycle used toner and ink cartridges.
- **Introduce** climate-appropriate potted plants to improve air quality and mood.
- **Use eco-friendly** caterers and cleaners. Team up with a plant-based catering company or one that intercepts and uses surplus food that would otherwise be binned. Companies can also sign up to a charity or food-waste app scheme to redistribute leftovers.
- **Provide mugs**, glasses, and fruit to dissuade employees from buying single-use plastic drinks or snacks. The average US employee goes through 500 disposable coffee cups a year.
- **If your company** runs a corporate gifting programme, source gifts from sustainable businesses, or donate to a charity instead.

Is digital working really greener than paper?

A paperless office saves trees, energy, and precious resources, but going digital isn't carbon-free. Digital documents, cloud storage, streaming, and other online activities have an impact.

Environmental concerns over paper aren't just about how many trees are used. Making paper is an energy-intensive business. Turning wood into paper requires heavy manufacturing, water, energy, and transportation. But while cutting out unnecessary use of paper in your workplace is a good idea, it's important to remember that electronic content also has an environmental impact. Digital documents are not carbon neutral.

We're only just beginning to understand the carbon cost of the ever-more enormous and power-hungry data centres that house our online content and "cloud" storage. It's estimated that the energy

---

A 2019 REPORT FOUND THAT **43%** OF **DATA CENTRES** DON'T HAVE AN **ENVIRONMENTAL POLICY**

---

usage of data centres will account for 3% of all carbon emissions by 2025, as our increasingly digital lives require yet more storage and processing power. By 2040, if current trends continue, storing our digital data will account for around 14% of global emissions – the equivalent CO_2 impact of the entire US today.

Decluttering both physically and virtually will reduce the environmental impact of your workday:

- **Streamline digital** systems, and review digital storage regularly, deleting documents you no longer need.
- **Many activities** that require the internet can be made greener: switch to an eco-friendly search engine that carbon-offsets the emissions that result from searches (such as by planting trees), and don't leave music or videos playing on your computer if you're not listening or watching.
- **Change your email** habits – see p.171 for more on this.
- **When you use** paper, print double-sided and in black and white, use scrap paper for notes and lists, and make sure you recycle everything.

What sort of paper is the most environmentally friendly?

Recycled paper saves trees from being cut down, but the story doesn't end there – there are other factors that contribute to the green credentials of paper.

Calculating the emissions involved in making paper involves looking at the life cycle of this energy-intensive production chain – from pulping to manufacturing practices, energy consumption, and transportation.

Using recycled paper – made from "post-consumer waste" – means you avoid supporting the use of pulp from virgin trees, thereby helping to reduce deforestation and the consequent loss of wildlife habitat.

While it may not be easy to establish a paper brand's total carbon footprint, the type of paper you choose can help you make a greener purchase:

- **Check how much** of the paper is recycled – there's no industry standard, so look for the highest percentage of post-consumer waste.
- **If possible, check** what kind of energy was used in the paper's production. Is the paper mill reliant on fossil fuels, or is it powered by alternative energy sources?
- **Look for FSC certification**. The Forest Stewardship Council promotes responsible management of the world's forests; FSC paper is sourced from mills that use sustainably managed forests and processes, where the welfare of indigenous people and those involved in the production process are protected. There is also an "FSC recycled" label, which guarantees that the paper is genuinely recycled.

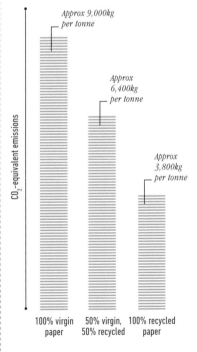

▲ The lower the percentage of virgin pulp used in paper, the lower the greenhouse gas emissions resulting from its manufacture.

"The internet has an impact: it already accounts for *nearly 4% of global carbon emissions.*"

What's the environmental impact of emails?

We send billions of emails daily with little thought, but our constant communication has an environmental price.

Each email has a carbon footprint: it takes electricity to type at your computer, to send the email through the network, and to store it in an inbox, which is managed by vast data centres around the world.

Sending one email can feel like a relatively low-impact activity, but the sheer volume of emails we collectively send has a sizeable effect. In 2019, a staggering 293.6 billion emails were sent each day, globally. The carbon emissions caused by the world's annual email output are equivalent to having an extra seven million cars on the roads. A 2019 study concluded that if each person in the UK sent one less email a day, national CO_2 emissions would be reduced by over 16,433 tonnes. And that's just the tip of the iceberg: streaming, which accounts for 60% of internet use, and data storage are also big sources of emissions.

Changing your mindset to prioritize what's good for the planet, even in such a small everyday action, makes a difference. Be selective and think before clicking "send". Are one- or two-word emails saying "Great, thanks" or "Okay" really necessary?

44,165 emails (the average number received in a year): 0.6 tonnes

Email with attachment: 50g

Text-only email: 4g

Spam email: 0.3g

▲ Your inbox's carbon footprint (measured in CO_2-equivalent emissions) depends on how many emails, and what kind, you receive. Spam, deleted unopened, has less of an impact.

Which are greener, e-books or physical books?

While e-readers are undeniably convenient, many people find printed books more immersive – but which has less of an environmental impact?

Both physical books and e-books have an environmental cost. The manufacture of each e-reader, required to read digital material, involves mining rare metals for the battery and screen, in addition to its cost in terms of fuel, water, and transportation. Printing a book requires paper, ink, water – it takes around 32 litres of water to produce a single book – and energy, used in production and shipping. In the UK alone, 191 million physical books were sold in 2018, using an enormous quantity of resources.

Which way of reading is greenest depends on the number of books you read. An e-reader needs to be used to read at least 25 books each year for the emissions produced in its manufacture to be less than the emissions that would be created by producing the same number of physical books. Most people keep an e-reader for around 4 years before updating it – so, if you know you don't read 100 books over 4 years, then physical books are the greenest option for you. If you're a regular reader, though, digital books are the more eco-friendly choice.

Keep the following in mind for more eco-friendly reading habits:

- **Resist upgrades** on e-readers and replace them only when necessary, making sure you recycle or sell on older models.
- **If you're sticking with** printed books, make use of your local library whenever possible (especially for children's books) and buy from – as well as donate and sell to – second-hand bookshops and charity or thrift shops.
- **Swap books** with friends, or organise a larger book exchange at work or in your local area, so everyone can find some new reading material without putting a burden on the planet. (That goes for this book, too!)

THE **AVERAGE PHYSICAL BOOK** GENERATES
7.5kg OF CO_2- EQUIVALENT EMISSIONS

IN 2019, **PRINT** ACCOUNTED FOR **85%** OF GLOBAL NEWS REVENUE

▶ Digital news is on the rise, but print remains popular, especially as literacy rates grow in areas of the world with less access to technology.

Is it okay to read printed newspapers and magazines?

A leisurely leaf through the weekend papers may be enjoyable, but printing them has a significant green cost.

Despite the decline of print media, the industry still gets through copious resources. In 2018, almost 374 million magazines and millions more newspapers were sold in the UK. Each required trees, energy, ink, and shipping. The printing process for glossy magazines results in the emission of volatile organic compounds (VOCs), which are toxic, and the shiny coating makes the paper harder to recycle. Many recycling centres don't accept them.

There are greener ways to keep up with the media:

- **Swap to news apps**, news sites, and digital versions of your favourite publications. They aren't carbon free, but they do have a lower eco-impact than printed matter.
- **Avoid picking up** free magazines and newspapers on your commute – free papers are often read for just a few minutes before being discarded.
- **If you are still** keen to support printed media, pass your copies on to friends, donate them, or use them for crafts after reading – then recycle them if you can.

How can I make my money do good for the planet?

Society relies on money to operate smoothly, but there is an increasing appreciation that how we choose to spend, save, and invest our money can work for or against the planet.

Each time you use your debit or credit card or part with your cash, you can make a consumer choice that goes some way, however small, to protecting the future of the planet. Many brands now seek international accreditation to signal that they consider the "three Ps" – people, planet, and profits. The accreditation B Corp, which requires businesses to change their legal governing documents to protect the three Ps, is the hardest to obtain.

Think about purchases in advance to ensure that your choices are environmentally sound.

Everyday banking

Until recently, the majority of banks invested in any industry that returned the most profit – from fossil fuels to armaments and mining companies. Today, more banks have an eye to the future and are keen to promote an ethical-investment ethos. Greener banks are transparent about their

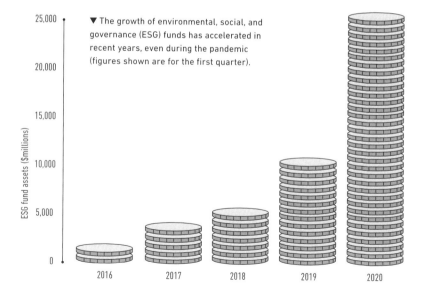

▼ The growth of environmental, social, and governance (ESG) funds has accelerated in recent years, even during the pandemic (figures shown are for the first quarter).

ESG fund assets ($millions)

25,000
20,000
15,000
10,000
5,000
0

2016   2017   2018   2019   2020

investments and prioritize lending to organizations with positive environmental and social goals, such as energy-efficient housing projects or charities.

Choose a bank that is based in your home country and is clear about what it invests in and which charities it works with. A transparent banking system helps promote a fairer society.

Ethical investment

Traditionally, stock exchanges have been packed with companies that trade in oil, weapons, and banking.

BETWEEN 2016 AND 2018, **GLOBAL SUSTAINABLE INVESTING** INCREASED BY **34%**

However, there is an emerging market of new investment products that work with ethical businesses only; this expanding sector is estimated to grow 173% by 2027. There are a number of green ways to invest:

- **If you've got** savings, shares, or pensions, take a closer look at what you have invested in. Think about which sectors you wish to support or avoid. Ethical funds or investing services can guide you to companies that fit your values. Look online for investment opportunities that prioritize environmental, social, and governance concerns, known as ESG investing.

- **If you are looking** to invest large sums, consider "angel" investing, where you invest directly (alone or in a group) into social enterprises and sustainably focused businesses.

- **Micro-financing**, or micro-loans, involve loaning small amounts of money to give entrepreneurs (often women) in developing countries a head start. Once the loan is repaid, it's used again for someone else, creating a circular system.

Insurance

As with banking and investment, ethical insurance is about making sure a company has an responsible and transparent investment policy. Try to favour companies that are clear about their investments (few are). Look out, too, for companies that are members of ClimateWise, a voluntary initiative whereby insurance companies commit to disclose their response to climate risk, raise climate awareness, and invest strategically for the environment.

Donating to charities

Setting aside some money for charity is a hugely worthwhile act. Faced with our planet's problems, it can be hard to choose who to support. If you're unsure, try supporting a smaller charity close to home. A little money goes a long way for a locally focused charity, and supporting a local issue helps to build a sense of community. You can also look for charities that appeal to the climate-related issues closest to your heart.

Which leisure activities are most damaging to the environment?

Sports enhance our health and wellbeing, but can also have ecological consequences. Keeping activities low-tech helps ensure that we mind the wellbeing of the planet, too.

Some popular leisure activities – particularly those that call for special equipment or require travel – have a significant impact on the environment.

Skiing

As well as involving travel and a lot of equipment, skiing has a hugely detrimental impact on the very mountains that make it so special: it compacts the soil and damages vegetation. Resorts are carbon heavy, with ski lifts and cable cars using up considerable amounts of energy. And shorter winter seasons due to climate change have led many resorts to manufacture artificial snow, using vast quantities of water.

Golf

The upkeep of pristine golf greens means that an average golf course uses 189 million litres of water a year. (The same amount would serve a village of 1,400 people for a year.)

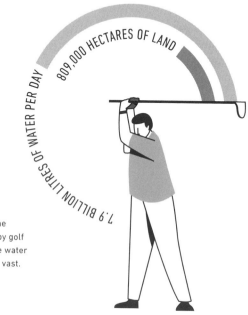

809,000 HECTARES OF LAND

7.9 BILLION LITRES OF WATER PER DAY

▶ Estimated figures for the amount of land taken up by golf courses in the US, and the water used to irrigate them, are vast.

The question as to whether overly manicured golf courses still act as wildlife spaces and carbon sinks is also debatable.

Surfing

Surfing may increase our respect of the ocean, but traditional surfboards and wetsuits are not eco-friendly. Neither can be recycled, which means that cheap foam or polystyrene boards that may be used for just one holiday can end up in landfill forever. In addition, most wetsuits are made of neoprene, which uses petroleum or other materials that have to be drilled for or mined.

Thinking about the impact of your chosen leisure activity can help you adopt greener practices:

- **If you do ski**, travel to the resort by train rather than by air.
- **If you're a keen** golfer, check out eco-friendly golf courses with sustainable water management, wildlife corridors, and solar-powered golf carts. Ask your local course what they're doing to sustain the land they are using.
- **If you need** equipment, look for plastic-free, biodegradable options, such as biodegradable rubber yoga mats, cork yoga blocks, and wooden surfboards. Choose natural materials over plastic.
- **Donate or sell** old equipment, and rent equipment whenever possible. There are plenty of rental platforms where you can obtain anything from skis to tents.

How can I be greener when I work out?

Getting fit and going green can go hand in hand. Multitask your exercise and ask more of your gym.

Electronic machines and heated rooms can mean your workout comes with a hefty energy-consumption tag. In addition, gym vending machines and snack bars are often full of foods and drinks in throwaway plastic packaging.

Keep exercise low-tech, and exercise outside, or at home, rather than inside a gym. Running, cycling, and outdoor circuit training are all low-impact options.

- **Swap gym classes** for outdoor boot camps or home workouts.
- **If you love the gym**, opt for classes where you work with your body weight rather than electronic equipment. Ask your gym where they source their electricity and whether they can cut down on single-use plastic. If you sense a lack of interest, consider swapping to a more eco-conscious gym.
- **Ditch grab-and-go** drinks and energy snacks. Carry a reusable water bottle and bring snacks from home.
- **Combine exercise** with litter picking, either at beach cleans or by "plogging", where you run and pick up litter at the same time.

FAMILY AND RELATIONSHIPS

What's the greenest form of contraception?

To go green from top to bottom, it's worth thinking about which method of birth control you use. Some have more of an impact on the environment, and on your health, than others.

When it comes to birth control, some of the most popular methods have potential negative side effects for the environment, as well as for users.

Impactful options

Most mainstream condoms are made from chemically enhanced latex. Latex itself is a natural product sourced from rubber trees (see p.131), but some of the chemicals in condoms, such as nonoxynol-9 (a spermicide) and parabens (a type of preservative) can have unwanted side effects for you and the environment. When brands promise extras such as a longer lasting experience, and enhanced pleasure and sensitivity, this generally means there are more chemicals. Studies suggest that some of these can disrupt hormones and vaginal flora. And when condoms end up in landfill, these chemicals can leach into the groundwater. Keep in mind, too, that most condoms also contain a milk protein called casein, which means that they aren't vegan. A further consideration is that this single-use product is thought to take thousands of years to biodegrade. With 9 billion condoms sold each year, that's a lot of latex languishing in landfill.

Hormonal oral contraception – "the pill" – is lower on waste, though it does have plastic packaging. Much of its eco-impact comes from the chemicals it contains, which pass through your body and into waterways. Studies show that synthetic oestrogen in the water affects egg production in fish, which in turn can disrupt marine ecosystems.

Several other contraceptives come with similar concerns. Both the ring and the patch are made of plastic and release hormones, as well as coming in plastic packaging – they need to be replaced monthly and weekly, respectively. A diaphram or cap can be reused for 2 years, is made of silicone, and contains no hormones, making it a less harmful option.

Greener methods

An IUD, or "coil", is a device that is inserted into the uterus and left in for an extended period of time. From an ecological perspective, this long-

565 CONDOMS WERE PICKED UP FROM NEW JERSEY BEACHES DURING A **2018 BEACH CLEAN**

lasting method produces little waste compared with other types of contraception. In addition, unlike the pill, IUDs release either no hormones or just a small amount of progestin, so have a negligible effect in terms of chemical hormones passing through the body into waterways.

Apps that help you track your ovulation to work out the best time to avoid getting pregnant may seem to have minimal environmental impact, but there is debate about how effective they are, with some studies recording a 27% failure rate.

There are plenty of eco-friendly contraception options out there; talk to your doctor if you are unsure.

• **Think about what's** right for you. Choosing a method of contraception is a personal decision, and the same option won't work for everyone, but if being green is top of your agenda, there are a few things to keep in mind (see table, below).

• **Consider long-lasting**, non-hormonal birth control options.

• **Look for condoms** that are biodegradable and, if necessary, vegan – some brands use natural latex and plant-based lubricants. Check whether the rubber was fairly traded and sustainably grown.

• **Don't flush** condoms down the loo; they clog up sewers, end up in the oceans, and can be ingested by marine animals and birds.

METHODS OF CONTRACEPTION

Condoms
Create lots of waste – even the biodegradable ones stick around for a long time – and often contain chemicals that can cause harm to humans and animals.

The pill
Creates some plastic waste, and causes hormones to enter the water supply, with potentially damaging long-term consequences for ecosystems and humans.

The coil / IUD
A low-waste, low-chemical option that works well for the planet, though implantation can be disruptive for the user.

"Making eco-friendly lifestyle changes is addictive – *encourage others to join you.*"

How can I make my sex life greener?

You may think the bedroom is one place you don't need to factor in environmental concerns, but there are plenty of sustainable swaps you can make to keep the fun eco-friendly.

Any sex-enhancing product you use, with your partner or alone, comes at a small cost to the planet. Commercial products are unlikely to be made from natural materials, and are not generally designed to be recycled. Many people use a lubricant to make sex or masturbation more comfortable and enjoyable, but most commercially produced lube contains the same chemicals found in condoms (see p.180), and comes packaged in plastic containers, which are usually unrecyclable.

Sex toys also pose environmental issues. Many are made of plastic and contain batteries (see p.140). Some sex-toy websites have recycling programmes, but in general used toys aren't recycled, as it is difficult to separate the component parts, particularly in the case of battery-operated vibrators. Most end up in landfill, where they break down over time into microplastics (see p.96) and silicone components. Silicone-only toys can be more easily recycled. Although its manufacture requires non-renewable petroleum and natural gases, silicone rarely breaks, and it is more inert than plastic, which means it leaches fewer chemicals into the ground if it does end up in landfill.

Looking for natural ingredients and simpler products can keep your green conscience clear:

- **Search for lubricants** that are not petroleum-based and don't contain chemicals such as parabens. Choose organic

ACCORDING TO ONE US SURVEY, **MORE THAN** **65%** OF WOMEN USE LUBE

products with natural and, if preferred, vegan, ingredients.
- **Try making** your own home-made lube. There are plenty of recipes online, using ingredients such as coconut oil or aloe vera.
- **When buying** sex toys, look for well-crafted, high-quality glass or wooden products over silicone ones. Failing this, do opt for silicone rather than plastic.
- **Go battery-free** – there are solar-powered vibrators on the market – and explore the new market of biodegradable vibrators.
- **Invest in a product** that's going to last for years, rather than break after a few enthusiastic sessions.

Can I have children and still be green?

Burgeoning population growth is one of the most pressing environmental issues today. For some, how to approach starting a family is a serious eco-dilemma.

Currently, the world's population is 7.8 billion, and that number is set to rise to 10.9 billion by 2100. With all those people putting increasing strain on the planet, having a child is one of the most carbon-emission-heavy things you can do.

In order to halt climate collapse, we need to reduce the amount of CO_2 generated per person to 2 tonnes a year by 2050. At the moment, Australians and Americans produce around 16 tonnes a year each, and the British 7 tonnes. The variation in per-capita impact is much more pronounced when industrialized countries are compared with poorer ones. Efforts to combat overpopulation can often feel aimed at the developing world, where populations are growing most rapidly, but it's the Western world's overconsumption of resources that has pushed our ecosystem to the brink. As the global population shoots up, our over-stretched resources will increasingly struggle to cope.

An ever-growing human population also brings us into conflict with animal species. A survey of land mammals found that almost half have lost 80% of their habitat in the last hundred years, as our expanding numbers compete with them for natural resources such as forests, water, and food.

For the climate-conscious, weighing up the decision to start a family against the added burden this means for the planet can be an immensely

CHILD IN A RICH COUNTRY
UP TO 16 TONNES/YEAR

 CHILD IN A DEVELOPING COUNTRY
0.07–0.1 TONNES/YEAR

◀ The average CO_2 emissions per capita across different countries in 2017 highlights the gulf between the carbon footprints of the rich and the poor.

emotional and difficult choice. For some, the answer is to not have children. "BirthStrike", a support group and political campaign set up in the UK in 2019, brings together people who have decided to remain childless because of the climate emergency. Other couples consciously commit to having just one child. A 2017 study calculated that by having one child fewer, a person in the developed world saves the equivalent of 58.6 tonnes of CO_2 each year (a figure that accounts for further descendents of that child), making this one of the most profound environmental steps you can take. However, if you do wish to start a family, there are options for lessening the eco-impact:

- **If you have children**, educate them on the responsibility they can take as they grow up to look after our Earth.
- **If you want a child** but are very concerned about the impact of adding another human to the planet, a possible option is to foster or adopt. In Australia, for example, each year 40,000 children seek new homes but only 0.5% are adopted. In the UK, over 8,000 more foster families are needed to meet the demand of children already in the care system.
- **Support organizations** that promote the education of girls in developing countries. Keeping girls in education in poorer countries encourages them to pursue careers, delay marriage and motherhood, and have fewer children.

Should I choose reusable nappies or disposables?

Disposable nappies are piling up in landfills, but reusables demand energy and water.

In the UK, 3 billion disposable nappies are used each year, with most babies getting through 4–6,000 nappies by the time they're potty trained. Most of these nappies end up in landfill, where they will take hundreds of years to decompose. Some are burnt as a source of fuel, but this adds to greenhouse-gas emissions.

Reusable nappies aren't always greener, though: one report found that the electricity used to wash them over 2.5 years accounts for 570kg of CO_2, while manufacturing enough disposable nappies for the same period of time produces only 550kg. If washed and dried responsibly, though, reusables will have a lesser impact overall.

- **Wash reusable nappies** at 30°C and hang them out to dry rather than using the tumble dryer.
- **If you're not sure** about reusable nappies, check out nappy "libraries", where you can try out various options before you buy.
- **Consider using** a combination of types – perhaps using disposables at night or when away from home.
- **Avoid baby wipes** for cleaning (see p.187).

Is it greener to make your own baby food?

Weaning can be a challenge at the best of times, and it may seem like an even larger mountain to climb if you are determined to feed your child as sustainably as possible.

As with other processed foods, baby food can have long supply chains, which translates into greater emissions from manufacture and transportation. Packaging is also an issue: single-serving pouches are convenient but rarely recyclable, adding to the world's single-use plastic problem.

Puréeing food yourself and introducing finger foods such as chopped fruit or pasta shapes allows you to take control over part of the production line. You'll also know exactly what ingredients are going into your baby's meals, so can avoid foods with large carbon or water footprints (see p.55).

If you do buy ready-made baby food, opt for greener brands, which are easy to find. In fact, we are more likely to choose organic when buying baby food than in the case of any other product. In the UK, just over half of all pre-made baby food is certified organic.

Here's how to help your little one eat green from day one:

- **Make your baby's** food from scratch as much as possible. Opt for seasonal fruit and veg, which is not only more eco-friendly but also higher in nutrients.
- **When you do** buy baby food, look for organic, locally produced options.
- **If buying pouches**, make sure they can be recycled, or be sent back to be recycled at source. You can also buy reusable pouches to fill with your own purée.

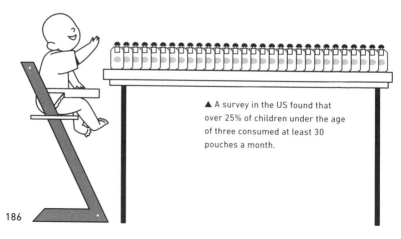

▲ A survey in the US found that over 25% of children under the age of three consumed at least 30 pouches a month.

How do I choose the most eco-friendly baby products?

Being green and finding the best toys and equipment for your baby go hand in hand. Move away from plastic and embrace a mix of traditional materials and new technology.

With a new baby, it can feel like there is no end to the items you suddenly need to buy, many of which can be damaging to the environment. A considerable number of these items are made of, or packaged in, plastic. Aside from the sourcing and disposal issues, the plastic often comes loaded with BPA (bisphenol A) and phthalates, which make it pliable so it can be moulded, but are thought to have toxic properties.

The same general issues that crop up regarding many other everyday items can also apply to baby products. Luckily, more eco-friendly alternatives are available than ever before:

- **There are non-plastic** versions of almost all baby essentials, from natural rubber dummies and steel or glass bottles with silicone teats to unbreakable crockery made from wood or silicone.
- **When it comes to** blankets, clothes, and other fabric items, aim to choose organic cotton or natural fibres over synthetic materials. For the greenest nappies, see p.185.
- **Choose organic** or non-synthetic ingredients when buying skincare products for babies, or raid your kitchen cupboards – there are endless recipes online for DIY "clean" skincare products that contain no artificial chemicals (see p.81 for more on skincare).
- **Swap single-use** wet wipes for reusable bamboo wipes or a cloth soaked in baby-safe tinctures or oils to help soothe skin irritation. If you do use

---

UP TO **85%** OF BABIES USE DUMMIES, MANY OF WHICH ARE **PLASTIC**

---

disposable wipes – when out and about, for instance – choose biodegradable, plastic-free ones, as most mainstream wipes break down into microplastics once thrown away.

- **Look for recycled** versions of everything you can think of, from pushchairs made of recycled materials to nappy bags made of plastic bottles.
- **Choose an organic** mattress for your baby's cot, and opt for cork play mats instead of spongy, brightly coloured plastic.

▼ Studies have shown that by the time the average child living in the UK is 10 years old, they will own this many toys.

2 3 8

Should I avoid plastic toys?

While single-use plastics rightfully receive a lot of negative media coverage, our kids' plastic toys might be an even bigger climate calamity.

The colourful world of kids' toys, where aggressive advertising piles pressure on parents to provide their child with the latest must-have item, is worth £74 billion globally each year. The number of toys owned by the average child has increased hugely in recent years – and most of them are quickly outgrown and discarded. Cheap and plentiful plastic toys have a whole host of downsides for the planet, as well as for children. Approximately 80% of the world's toys are produced in China; often, factory conditions are less than eco-friendly, and sending these products around

the globe clocks up air miles. Many toys also come in excessive plastic packaging, which ends up in landfill.

Plastic toys often can't be recycled. Many also contain other components such as metal, which means it's hard for the elements to be separated out by recycling facilities. Like all plastics, plastic toys have a numbering system that indicates whether or not they can be recycled (see p.25).

Many plastic toys are made from polyvinyl chloride (PVC), which contains numerous chemical additives. Chemicals of particular concern found in some plastics are phthalates and bisphenol A (BPA), which are hormone disrupters; in the EU they are now banned from items that children chew or suck on. Some plastic toys may even contain traces of heavy metals.

Here's how to ensure your child's fun is harmless for both them and the planet:

- **Opt for toys** made of wood, or recycled or low-impact materials such as cardboard.
- **Be wary of** second-hand plastic toys, as they may not meet current safety standards.
- **Buy fewer toys** from the outset. As well as reducing consumption, studies show that this benefits children, as those with fewer toys

---

90% OF ALL CHILDREN'S TOYS **ARE PLASTIC**

---

play with them for longer and use their imagination more than those with an abundance of toys. Place more focus on books and crafts, to balance your child's playtime.

- **Look into toy** rental companies, where you can borrow toys for 6 months and then swap them for new ones to meet your child's changing needs as they develop.
- **Pass on or donate** old toys rather than sending them to landfill.
- **For well-meaning** friends and family, gently suggest alternatives to plastic toys (see p.126).

What's the best way of recycling things my child has grown out of?

With overconsumption rife in the developed world, finding ways to pass on children's items to others is key.

From baby equipment to children's clothes and toys, having a child means endlessly clearing out clutter and accumulating more as your child grows. There are plenty of ways to ensure your child's possessions carry on being useful once they've been outgrown:

- **Online marketplaces** such as eBay, Facebook, and other sites allow you to sell on toys, clothes, and some equipment.
- **Create chains** of friends and family, where you all pass on clothes, books, and toys to each other as your respective children grow.
- **Donate children's** clothes and toys to charities.
- **Look into companies** who rent out bundles of age-appropriate clothes or boxes of toys.
- **Get in touch** with local nurseries, playgroups, and schools, who are often happy to take old toys and books that are in good condition.

Is it green to have a pet?

For many of us, pets are a cherished part of our lives, but pet ownership often comes at a cost to the planet. Being aware of this can help you reduce your pet's carbon pawprint.

Pet ownership is popular – in 2020, it was estimated that 67% of US households owned some kind of pet. Owning a dog, cat, or other type of pet brings many clear benefits, whether that is the daily exercise dog owners enjoy, or the companionship, comfort, and boost to mental health that animals provide. However, in the US, for example, keeping pets is thought to contribute 64 million tonnes of CO_2 and methane to the environment each year. That's the equivalent of putting another 13.6 million cars on the roads.

Our pets' needs

Pets' food (see p.192) and the resources needed to keep them warm, safe, and happy, all have an ecological impact. Many pets have a meat-heavy diet, at a time when we all need to reduce our reliance on the meat industry (see pp.34–37). The food our dogs and cats eat is thought to account for a quarter of the greenhouse-gas emissions from animal agriculture. How we dispose of the waste from dogs and cats – using dog-poo bags and cat litter – also takes its toll (see p.193).

Domestic cats also pose a significant risk to wildlife, with serious concerns that they are leading to declines in bird numbers. In the UK, it's estimated that free-roaming pet cats kill 275 million prey animals a year, 27 million of which are birds.

For fish owners, keeping tanks running demands energy. Typically, fish tanks are getting bigger, and a rise in the popularity of tropical fish species means that tanks for these need to be kept warmer, which requires yet more energy. In addition, there's a question mark over the sustainability of taking these fish out of their natural habitat.

Non-native pets

There is also wider concern about the growing numbers of exotic species, such as monkeys and tropical birds, that are removed from their natural habitats to be kept as pets. This practice is often illegal and frequently cruel. The sudden fashion for otters as pets in the Far East, for example, has lead to the adults being poached in the wild

DOMESTIC CATS ARE CLASSED AS THE
3rd MOST THREATENING INVASIVE SPECIES

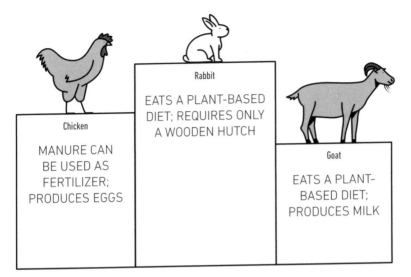

▲ Studies have found these animals to make the most eco-friendly pets.

Chicken

MANURE CAN BE USED AS FERTILIZER; PRODUCES EGGS

Rabbit

EATS A PLANT-BASED DIET; REQUIRES ONLY A WOODEN HUTCH

Goat

EATS A PLANT-BASED DIET; PRODUCES MILK

so their young can be sold as cute pets. Many exotic pets are kept in captivity before being shipped to their destination, and some don't survive the journey.

While not owning a pet at all – reducing the demand for breeding them – is the greenest option here, there are ways for those of us who have pets, or who would like a pet, to make pet ownership more eco-friendly:

- **If you want** a dog or cat, get in touch with an animal rescue centre rather than buying a kitten or puppy from a pet shop or breeder. In the UK, tens of thousands of rescued dogs and cats are rehomed every year.

- **Use sustainable** sources of cat litter or sawdust, such as wood chips or plant-based materials (see p.193).
- **Make your pet's** diet as eco-friendly as possible (see p.192).
- **Avoid chemical-laden** pet shampoos and treatments as much as possible.
- **Choose non-plastic** pet toys, and consider buying pet beds, bowls, leads, and other items second-hand from auction sites if they are in good condition.
- **Remember, it's not** green – or, in most cases, kind – to keep exotic animals.

What are the greenest forms of pet food?

Feeding our dogs and cats is adding to the burden of meat production on the planet, but it is possible to make greener choices when stocking up on pet food.

Pet food is responsible for a staggering 25% of the resources – the land, animals, and energy – involved in meat production. Where your dog's or cat's food comes from and how it's made translates into its environmental cost. Cheaper brands that use mass-produced meat (see pp.36–37) have a hugely negative impact on the environment, just as cheap, overly processed food brands do. At the other end of the spectrum, premium or "gourmet" brands often contain meat that would be considered acceptable as human food, which misses an opportunity to use up offal and other less appetizing cuts, reducing waste.

Can dogs and cats be vegetarian?

Dogs produce the enzyme amylase, needed to digest starch, which means that they can eat cereal-based food and in theory should be able to tolerate a vegetarian diet. It is possible to find vegan and vegetarian dog foods, but these need to be considered carefully, as your dog needs a range of proteins and vitamins to stay healthy. One study found that a quarter of vegetarian dog foods didn't contain adequate vital nutrients. Cats are unavoidable carnivores and cannot survive on a vegetarian or vegan diet.

ACCORDING TO ONE ESTIMATE, **52%** OF CATS...

...AND UP TO **59%** OF DOGS ARE OVERFED

To limit the eco impact of your pet's diet:

- **If you have a dog**, consider feeding it a mixed meat and vegetable diet.
- **Keep abreast of** innovations such as dog food made of insects or

---

---

lab-grown meat (see p.37), which are coming onto the market. Some of these still have environmental implications, but could offer better solutions in the future.

- **If you have a cat**, choose organic food or brands that are clear about the kind of meat they use.
- **Buy food in tins**, which are easiest to recycle, or dry food in compostable bags.

What do I do about poo bags and cat litter?

All of those plastic poo bags and mountains of cat litter are far from green. We need to find better solutions.

The average dog owner gets through around 1,000 poo bags a year. "Biodegradable" poo bags exist, and are preferable to standard plastic, but be wary of the claim. Some of these bags don't actually decompose at all, while others take decades.

Clay-based cat litter is produced via "strip mining". This process removes the topsoil to reach the layer of clay, destroying vegetation, causing habitat loss and mineral depletion, and adding to the risk of flooding. Crystal-based cat litter also involves mining and may contain carcinogenic substances.

- **If you're in the** countryside, use a stick to flick your dog's poo into the bushes, making sure it doesn't end up near a waterway or path.
- **Choose corn-starch** poo bags, which decompose most successfully.
- **If you have a garden**, one option is to invest in a machine that turns dog poo into fertilizer. Home composting of dog poo is not recommended because of the disease-carrying bacteria it contains.
- **Avoid indoor litter trays**, or use litter made from natural substances, such as woodchip or paper.

How can I be green when I die?

It might not be the cheeriest of topics, but the conversation around green burials is an important one, as more and more people look for ways to limit their burden on the Earth.

The space needed for burials is a growing issue, which may be one of the reasons why more and more people – including just over 50% of Americans – are choosing cremation over burials. However, each cremation releases 400kg of CO_2 into the atmosphere, adding to the atmospheric load of greenhouse gases. While burials don't contribute carbon emissions directly, they have other eco-impacts in addition to requiring space beneath the ground. One major concern is that the toxins from embalming fluids, and chemicals from medical treatments such as chemotherapy, leach into the soil surrounding the coffin over time.

A HUMAN BODY TAKES ONLY **30** **DAYS** TO FULLY DECOMPOSE IN A **COMPOST BURIAL CHAMBER**

Other, more eco-friendly, options are available. In 2017, 10% of burials in the UK employed alternative methods, and this number is rising as people are seeking greater control over the environmental impact of their funeral. Spending a little time thinking about the choices you have, and sharing your wishes with your nearest and dearest, can help ensure you have a greener end of life.

Eco coffins and natural burials

Natural burials are gaining popularity. These avoid chemical preservatives or embalming fluids, and use coffins and caskets made from sustainably sourced biodegradeable materials, such as cardboard, willow, or wicker, which allow the body to break down naturally and quickly.

These burials are often accompanied by woodland funerals, which take place in forests or other natural areas. Services can be carried out at a separate location from the burial site, if desired, by a religious or non-religious celebrant. In place of traditional gravestones – made from materials such as marble and granite, which need to be mined – trees or small pieces of slate can be positioned to act as a marker or memento. This low-impact option allows people to be buried in a way that is more integrated with nature than in traditional cemeteries. Loved ones have a special place to come back to, and the cost of the funeral goes towards the conservation of the land.

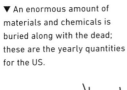

▼ An enormous amount of materials and chemicals is buried along with the dead; these are the yearly quantities for the US.

73,000 KM
OF HARDWOOD
BOARDS

53,000 TONNES
OF STEEL

1.4 MILLION TONNES
OF CONCRETE

3.1 MILLION LITRES OF
FORMALDEHYDE

Alternative burials

"Composting" burials are gradually being introduced in the US, Australia, and other countries. Here, woodchip and living plant material are used to help break down the body efficiently, transforming it into soil in just over a month. In the UK and the US, some companies are using a method called "resomation", or "water cremation", whereby the body is dissolved in an alkaline liquid in a matter of hours, leaving bone ash, which can be given to loved ones; the fluid is sent to a waste-treatment plant afterwards.

Other greener end-of-life practices

Families of loved ones can request a "bio urn", or "living urn", made from a biodegradable material such as bamboo. Cremated ashes are placed in the bottom of the urn and a growth mix is added on top, into which a young tree is planted. The urn is then buried, and decomposes as the tree grows.

Instead of floral tributes (see p.123), many families ask mourners to donate to a chosen charity. Mourners can also be asked to offset the emissions of funeral cars, travel, and wakes to honour the wishes of the deceased. There are eco-friendly funeral directors who can help advise on these options.

TRAVEL AND TRANSPORT

Which is the greenest mode of transport?

School runs, shopping trips, and daily commutes all add up, so choose your vehicle wisely – two wheels are better than four, and trains are your best bet for longer distances.

Transport is one of the biggest contributors to global greenhouse-gas emissions, responsible as a whole for around 14% of total emissions. Many of us regularly make choices about how we get around, so this is one area where individuals acting in a greener way can really make a difference.

If you're travelling only a short distance, it goes without saying that walking trumps all other modes of transport. Riding a bike also creates zero emissions, and you can reduce the environmental impact of buying a bike by choosing a brand made in your home country, to cut down on air miles. Electric bikes and scooters are a little more complicated – see opposite for more on these.

Conscience over comfort

Petrol and diesel buses, on average, produce about 1.3kg of CO_2 per kilometre travelled, but their

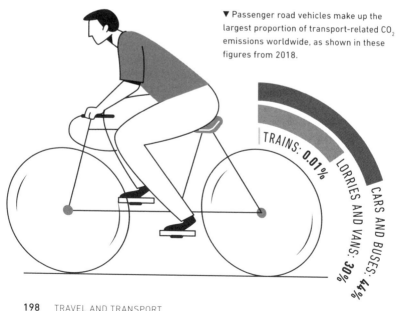

▼ Passenger road vehicles make up the largest proportion of transport-related CO_2 emissions worldwide, as shown in these figures from 2018.

TRAINS: 0.01%

LORRIES AND VANS: 30%

CARS AND BUSES: 44%

efficiency depends on how many people are on the bus. While a bus is nearly always better than a single person in a petrol or diesel car, if the car is transporting four people then it has lower carbon emissions per person than the average bus. Trains are the greenest form of public transport. They can be diesel or electric but increasingly are the latter, though it does vary across different countries. Germany aims to have 70% of its network

---

AN ELECTRIC TRAIN EMITS
80% LESS CO$_2$ PER
KILOMETRE THAN A CAR

---

electrified by 2025, Switzerland is already at 100%, and the UK sits at 42%.

So, depending on the distance you're travelling, and who or what you need to bring with you, you have a few low-impact options. For long journeys, electric train is best, followed by coach. For mid-range journeys, the greenest option is a train, then a full car, then a bus. A solo driver in a car is the second-worst option, with the worst of all being plane travel (see pp.206–207).

- **If you're able to**, walk or cycle to your destination.
- **Take the train** when you can.
- **If you have to drive**, see if there is any chance of car-sharing with a friend or colleague (see p.205).

Are electric bikes and scooters eco-friendly?

In many cities there's been a huge rise in the popularity of e-bikes and e-scooters, but they're not carbon neutral.

An electric scooter seems like a great green option to cut down on the CO$_2$ emissions of a commute. E-bikes too have gained massively in popularity; in Australian cities, for instance, they have tripled in number over the last few years. An electric bike has a range of around 80km per charge, while some new scooters can keep going for up to 128km.

Add in the raw materials, production, and shipping, however, and the picture gets more complex: a recent study in the US proved that e-bikes and e-scooters fall behind buses, walking, and non-electric cycling when their whole life cycle is taken into account. Then there are the batteries: as is the case with electric cars (see p.202), motor-driving batteries are energy- and resource-intensive to produce and difficult to dispose of. What's more, the energy used to charge them doesn't necessarily come from renewable sources.

If it's a choice between an e-bike or e-scooter and a car, pick the bike or scooter. But if you're comparing them with walking or non-electric cycling, electric options aren't greener.

Which modes of transport cause the least pollution in cities?

How green city travel is depends partly on the initiatives taken by local authorities to reduce emissions, but your personal choices do count.

The air quality of our cities is an ever-present issue. As well as adding to the global climate emergency, carbon emissions in cities have meant toxic levels of air pollution for inhabitants. We're only beginning to understand the full effect that this has on our bodies. While the effects on respiratory health are well documented – with children and the elderly especially vulnerable – increasingly, studies are finding that air pollution also impacts cognitive health and plays a role in our susceptibility to Covid-19. Drastically cutting down our urban pollution is key to our long-term health, and a critical step in fighting climate change.

Greener cities

Forward-thinking cities are investing in electric or carbon-neutral public transport systems, as well as installing

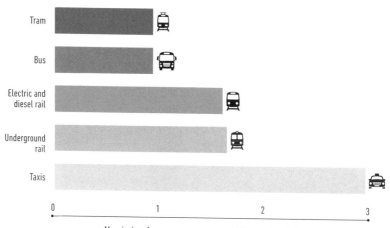

Megajoules of energy per passenger, per kilometre travelled

▲ This data shows the energy efficiency of various modes of transport, when used to maximum capacity. More efficient vehicles – combined with renewably sourced energy – means fewer emissions.

more cycling lanes. A range of other initiatives are also being taken, from car-free days to more pedestrian areas, putting in place lower emissions zones, and increasing support for lower emission and emission-free transport.

At a personal level, walking, cycling, and being mindful about the eco pros and cons of public transport are the greenest things you can do.

- **Walking and cycling** produce zero emissions at street level.

- **Trams** are one of the greenest forms of public transport when factors such as the average length of trips and the number of passengers are taken into account. Electric trams emit no fumes and networks that use renewable energy are particularly green.

- **Buses**, when they run efficiently, follow narrowly behind trams; the most eco-friendly buses transport large numbers of people, provide accessible and in-demand routes, and have moved, or are moving towards, sustainable sources of energy. In the UK, the London bus fleet introduced its first hybrid engines in 2006, with electric- and hydrogen-powered buses following. Many European countries are also moving to hydrogen-powered buses.

- **Underground train** or subway networks run just behind buses on the environmental scale, though they can be polluting for the passengers using them. In major cities, they are designed to transport a high density of people to their destination quickly. In London, for instance, prior to Covid-19, 3–4 million people used the underground each day; the system is looking at more sustainable fuel options, such as harnessing the power from its brakes to recycle energy.

- **Fleets of "green" taxis** using zero- or low-emission cars are now operating in some cities and towns. There's an ongoing debate about the environmental impact of on-demand taxi apps, which often take people off public transport or encourage them to take a taxi rather than walk or cycle (a 2018 report in the US found that 60% of people surveyed said this was the case). Taxi apps have also added to the number of cars on the road, increasing congestion in cities, which in turn slows down non-electric vehicles and creates more air pollution. If you're using a taxi app, choose the car-pool option.

- **River ferries** can seem like a good way to get around a city, but their eco-efficiency depends on the fuel source they use and how they're regulated. In cities where ferries run mostly on fossil fuels, they can emit around 100 times more emissions than cars. In Europe, more and more cities are investing in electric ferries for commuters and developing longer routes as an alternative to getting in the car, making ferries an increasingly eco-friendly choice.

How green are electric cars?

Electric cars are touted as the green transport revolution, but how clean they are partly depends on how they are made, and where the energy that powers them comes from.

Making up 10% of new car registrations in the UK, electric cars are seen as an aspirational solution to the climate crisis. However, estimates of the emissions caused by electric cars vary considerably, and depend on many assumptions. One report has estimated the emissions from an electric car over its full life cycle to be one-third of those from a petrol or diesel car.

The manufacture of any car has a carbon cost; in the case of electric cars, a big part of this is from the battery. Making traction batteries, which power electric motors, is an incredibly emission-heavy process. Making an electric car creates, on average,

---

IT'S PREDICTED THAT **BY 2050** THE CO_2 EMISSIONS OF **EUROPE'S ELECTRIC CARS** WILL GO DOWN BY 73%

8.8 tonnes of CO_2 compared with 5.6 tonnes for a petrol car. Once in use, a fully electric car produces no carbon emissions directly (in the form of exhaust fumes), but it still produces air-polluting particles from brake and tyre dust. And when it

comes to charging, electric cars are only as green as the electricity used to power the battery. Ideally, this should come from a renewable source; as renewable energy becomes more widespread (see pp.134–35), electric cars will become greener.

Not all electric cars are equal. Emissions vary for hybrids, "range extenders", and fully electric vehicles:

- **A fully electric car** charges its battery from the mains. If it uses renewable energy, this produces zero emissions from driving.

- **A range extender** has a small back-up engine to power the battery when it runs low, so you can drive further before recharging. The slightly smaller batteries used for these cars can lessen the eco-impact of their production, but, in most cases, a combustion engine powered by fossil fuels is still used.

- **A hybrid** has both a normal combustion engine and a traction battery, which stores energy from braking and from the engine at higher speeds. Some hybrids can also be plugged in to charge the battery. The extra weight reduces the efficiency of the car, so at higher speeds the battery runs down quite quickly.

Which is greener, using the air con or driving with the windows down?

Whether or not air conditioning is the greenest way to cool down depends on when you use it.

Your car's air con is powered by the battery, which in turn is recharged via the engine in a petrol or diesel car. Using air con increases your fuel consumption (or uses more battery charge in an electric car). However, driving with the windows down creates drag at higher speeds, which slows the car down so that it needs to draw on more fuel to maintain its speed. Both options decrease fuel efficiency, so which should you pick?

The answer depends on the speed you're travelling at. On fast roads, fuel efficiency relies on your car being as aerodynamic as possible, making it greener to use air con. In urban areas, on the other hand, winding down the window is the better option. On short trips, air con can reduce fuel economy by up to 25% in very hot temperatures. Here's what to keep in mind:

- **At speeds below** 55mph it's generally more fuel-efficient to have the windows down; above 55mph, air con is greener.
- **Open car doors** and windows before getting in, to get rid of hot air.
- **Switch off** the air con when you're in traffic, if possible, to reduce energy consumption.
- **Park in the shade** when you can.

What's the greenest option when thinking about buying a new car?

While the most eco-friendly choice is not to have a car at all, if you want to carry on driving, now's the time to embrace electric or to start to make plans to switch over.

Although electric cars have a big carbon cost from their manufacture (see p.202), the extra emissions from the production of a new electric car compared with a petrol or diesel car will be cancelled out by its in-use emissions savings in less than 2 years.

A second-hand hybrid or electric car can also be a good choice: although battery lifespan is a consideration with electric cars, most come with decent manufacturers' warranties of around 5–8 years. A new petrol car is generally more fuel-efficient than an older petrol model, but buying another fossil-fuelled car is the least green option. With many countries banning them over the next decade or so, we need to start moving away from these vehicles.

Hiring cars

If you want to cut down your car use altogether, not owning a car and hiring one when you really need to

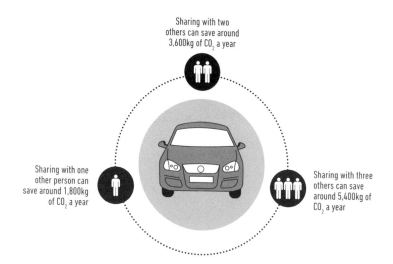

Sharing with two others can save around 3,600kg of CO_2 a year

Sharing with one other person can save around 1,800kg of CO_2 a year

Sharing with three others can save around 5,400kg of CO_2 a year

▲ The more people car-share, the more CO_2 emissions are reduced.

can be a good solution. This is also likely to encourage you to walk, cycle, or take the train or bus more. Some cities operate short-term hire schemes with electric car fleets.

Sharing cars

Carpooling schemes are not new; however, while some countries have carpooling lanes in place to encourage this practice, in other places it hasn't caught on. Nonetheless, carpooling is a great idea, reducing traffic congestion and changing our habits regarding vehicle dependency. Sharing your ride with others will significantly reduce greenhouse-gas emissions.

Today, real-time carpooling apps help you pair up with fellow travellers and share the cost. If you feel safe using them, these offer a convenient and emission-light solution for travel.

Cutting down car use as much as possible is key as we work towards a greener world:

- **Evaluate whether** you really need to use the car as often as you do, or whether you could get by without one altogether.
- **If you hire** a car for a longer journey, choose a hybrid or electric option if available; failing that, choose an economy petrol model rather than a gas-guzzling SUV.
- **If you're buying** a new car to replace one that will no longer be on the road (and if money is no barrier), then the most environmentally friendly option is to buy a new electric car.

Is it better to idle in traffic or to stop and restart?

Idling a petrol or diesel engine for a few moments may seem harmless, but this habit isn't at all green.

Air pollution is one of the biggest environmental issues and one that is set to worsen in the coming years, as our urban areas grow. Keeping your engine running when stationary adds to this pollution, with implications for everyone's health. Car exhaust fumes are not only toxic but also mainly consist of greenhouse gases.

The situation here is quite simple. Idling your engine while stationery for more than 10 seconds uses more energy and emits more greenhouse gases then stopping and starting the engine. The cumulative effect of this has a definite impact: for every 10 minutes you turn off the engine instead of idling, you save half a kilogram of CO_2. Thankfully this is one habit that's easy to cut:

- **Turn off the engine** when you stop the car. Many newer models of car do this automatically.
- **Switch to** an electric car to eliminate the issue of street-level pollution altogether (see p.202).

Should I give up flying?

While not flying at all is the greenest way to go, if this isn't possible, there are still measures you can take to help to reduce your impact when you fly.

In 2019, the global aviation industry accounted for 2% of greenhouse-gas emissions. Though this is less than, say, the global car industry, this figure has been on a rising trajectory, as air travel has become more and more common in an increasingly globalized world. One person's CO_2 emissions from a flight between New York and London is more than the average person in a developing country produces in a year. While some airlines are working on alternatives to fossil fuels and developing electric planes for short-haul flights, aviation is a long way off being carbon neutral.

250kg OF CO$_2$-EQ, ON AVERAGE, IS EMITTED PER HOUR OF FLYING

A growing trend

Giving up flying and swapping to slow or domestic travel is the best way to bring down your own personal emissions, eclipsing most other measures to be greener. In countries where it's common to fly multiple times a year, the trend to move away from flying is gathering traction: 23% of Swedes have reduced the number of flights they take each year due to "flygskam" – "flight shame" – attributed in part to climate activist Greta Thunberg's insistence on not flying, which has inspired a new generation of people to rediscover the joy of slow travel. However, for many people, work commitments or visiting family who live abroad mean that speedy travel is sometimes unavoidable.

During the lockdown in early 2020, flights reduced by 90% – something which climate activists only months earlier had assumed to be impossible. As a result, air pollution cleared in urban areas, birds flourished, and many people reassessed the need to fly, especially for business travel, taking into account the public-health risks and potential disruptions. Many airports are no longer expanding, which is a big win for the environment locally and global CO_2 emissions. But will these changes in our behaviour persist?

If you decide not to fly, or want to cut back:

- **Share your pledge** via social media to encourage others.
- **For holidays**, choose destinations closer to home rather than long-haul, and put thought and heart into planning your journey via train, ferry, bike, coach, or car.

THERE WERE ALMOST
39 million
FLIGHTS IN 2019

25% OF EMISSIONS ARE FROM LANDING AND **take-off**

IN 2014, **15%** OF THE UK'S POPULATION
TOOK **70%** OF THE UK'S FLIGHTS

- **Take fewer, but longer** holidays, so you can build in an extended travel period. For example, swap a few mini breaks for a one- or two-week trip, and travel by train. To minimize your impact if and when you do have to fly:
- **Offset your carbon emissions**. Your airline may offer this as part of the booking process, but if not, it's never been easier to personally offset. Tree planting is one of the most popular ways to offset, and there has been a rise in consumer-friendly, tree-planting apps that offer real-time updates of the trees you plant. Choose your scheme carefully, however, as there has been some controversy surrounding this area (see pp.208–209).
- **Choose a greener airline**. Not all planes produce the same emissions. Factors such as passenger capacity and the type of aircraft will affect a flight's eco-impact. There are online calculators that compare airlines and plane types to help you choose. The more demand there is for greener airlines, the faster the wider industry will respond.
- **Fly direct**: a larger proportion of emissions are released on take-off compared with the rest of a flight, so if you're flying long-haul, opt for the journey with the fewest legs.
- **Travel light**. The heavier the plane, the more emissions it emits, so cut down on your luggage, especially if flying short-haul. Think minimal clothes, fewer toiletries, and swap paper for digital books if possible.
- **Fly economy class** – the more people on the plane, the better the use of space, and the fewer planes needed overall.

Does carbon offsetting really work?

Carbon offsetting may sound complicated, but the practice is becoming more accessible. For offsetting to be really worthwhile, it's important to approach it with the right mindset.

Carbon offsetting – compensating for CO_2 emissions by funding actions that counter them – seems like a great idea, but in practice has proved problematic. It is often associated with polluting businesses who use it as a smokescreen, claiming they are carbon neutral by offsetting more than the emissions they produce, then continuing to plan for unrestricted growth. Offsetting isn't a get-out-of-jail-free card to carry on as normal; rather, it is a tool to be used in addition to reducing your carbon footprint. The best-case scenario would be to stop generating emissions or polluting altogether, but in the real world we need offsetting, and more of us need to do it.

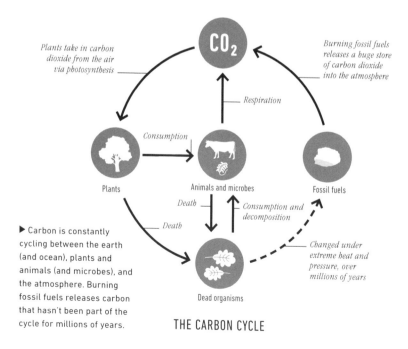

Plants take in carbon dioxide from the air via photosynthesis

Burning fossil fuels releases a huge store of carbon dioxide into the atmosphere

Respiration

Consumption

Plants

Animals and microbes

Fossil fuels

Death

Consumption and decomposition

Death

Changed under extreme heat and pressure, over millions of years

Dead organisms

▶ Carbon is constantly cycling between the earth (and ocean), plants and animals (and microbes), and the atmosphere. Burning fossil fuels releases carbon that hasn't been part of the cycle for millions of years.

THE CARBON CYCLE

Although the number of people who offset is still small, offsetting is a growing trend. In 2019, only 1% of air travellers carbon-offset their journeys – but this figure has grown 140-fold since 2008, as offsetting has become easier.

How does it work?

Offsetting doesn't directly cancel out the effects of the emissions created by, say, your holiday, but it does help to reduce the total amount of emissions globally.

There is debate over the best way to offset emissions, which schemes to invest in, and how much to offset. Options include contributing to the cost of planting trees, investing in renewable energy sources such as wind and solar, or funding projects to reduce deforestation or provide fuel-efficient cooking stoves, solar cookers, or clean drinking water. Trees will act as a carbon sink for decades to come and absorb rising levels of carbon dioxide, making them one of our best defences against climate change.

Now is the time to get involved:

- **Use an offsetting app** or calculator – they make it easy to navigate your way through the offsetting options, not just for flying but for every aspect of your life.
- **Choose offsetting** organizations that are verified by independent accreditation or that can share calculations of their impacts from previous years.

- **Check that the company** you wish to offset with is transparent about the project you will be funding, where it is, and what the goal is. They should also share regular updates on how it's progressing, either on their website or directly with you. Look for companies that employ and help local people in the regions in which they work. If you choose to invest in trees, seek out

---

BETWEEN 2018 AND 2019, ONE ACCREDITOR REPORTED A **300%** INCREASE IN THE NUMBER OF **INDIVIDUALS BUYING OFFSETS**

---

schemes that plant varieties that are the most effective carbon sinks, in locations where they aren't displacing indigenous people.

- **If you need** a quick and easy option, buy "certified carbon offsets" – financial certificates sold to fund wind and solar projects.

"Changing our attitudes to travel is crucial *to the fight against climate breakdown.*"

Where's the greenest place to go on holiday?

How far you travel, where you visit, and when you go can make the difference between your holiday being green or an environmental hazard.

In 2019, a total of 1.4 billion people went on holiday. Some parts of the world are visited more than others. The term "overtourism" describes the situation in which a popular destination is flooded with so many tourists that it has a negative impact on the environment and the people who live there – think Venice or Machu Picchu. Overtourism can cause housing shortages, damage to infrastructure, and increased litter and pollution, as well as putting strain on water supplies.

"Undertourism" describes the opposite scenario, in which a region is able to cope with visitor numbers. Plan your next holiday wisely to ease the pressure on popular areas:

- **Visit lesser-known** destinations rather than bucket-list attractions or social-media highlights – or explore your home country.
- **Holiday out of season**; as well as avoiding school holidays, consider going away in winter.
- **Be considerate** of locals and their way of life.

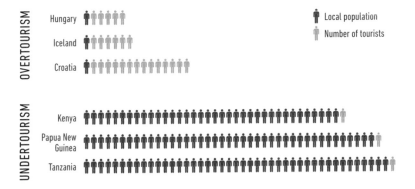

▲ On a measure of tourism density, here represented by ratio of locals to tourists at peak holiday times, these countries are at each end of the extreme.

What is ecotourism and why is it important?

We don't need to stop travelling altogether to reduce our travel footprint; by being more Earth-conscious when we do travel, we can make a difference.

Tourism has been an enormous industry, accounting for 1 in 10 of all jobs globally in 2019. It also accounted for 8% of the greenhouse gases generated by human activity.

There are ways to travel more sustainably, though. As responsible tourists, we all want to ensure that our holiday or adventure of a lifetime doesn't harm the environment any more than it has to. Ecotourism takes this further: instead of just limiting your impact, your holiday actually makes a positive contribution to the area you're visiting. It's about using tourism to help people and the planet.

There are a range of ways in which you can make your next holiday as green as it can be:

- **Use the holiday** as a chance to spend more time in nature – enjoy camping, glamping, cycling, or walking holidays.
- **Make the journey** part of the adventure and embrace slow travel, getting around by train or bike.
- **Respect "leave no trace"** signs in forests, beaches, and other natural environments. Dispose of litter appropriately – ideally, take it home with you, leaving the area unchanged by your visit.

ONE REPORT FOUND THAT **87%** OF HOLIDAY-MAKERS WANT TO **TRAVEL SUSTAINABLY**

- **Seek out activities** that help fund local schemes; for example, a bike tour that funds a local conservation project.
- **Make sure** your accommodation has plastic-free policies (see opposite), gives back to local initiatives, and supports the local economy. Choose eco-hotels over big chains.
- **Use your holiday** to learn a new practical green skill, such as by going on a permaculture course.
- **Be wary of volunteering** holidays. You may have the best of intentions, but volunteering programmes often aren't accredited, and swooping in to help build a school for a week might be taking jobs away from local people, as well as not being the best use of scant resources.

How can I use less plastic on holiday?

Avoiding plastic when you're outside your usual routine and travelling can be a challenge. A little forward planning is key to enjoying a plastic-free break.

Our plastic-free intentions can fly out the window once we're away from home, resulting in an increase in our consumption of single-use plastic. Fortunately, there are some easy ways to avoid a holiday plastic binge:

- **Make sure you pack** your reusable shopping bag, water bottle, and coffee cup to carry around on holiday. Make a point of asking for tap water (in countries where it is safe to drink) or filtered water, rather than bottles. If safe drinking water isn't available, invest in a SteriPEN or pack water-sterilizing tablets.
- **Add a reusable cutlery set** – try sustainably sourced bamboo – to your bag, for picnics and eating while travelling.
- **Resist the mini toiletries** in hotels and pack a plastic-free toiletries kit. Choose toothpaste tabs, bamboo cotton buds, and solid shampoo and shower-gel bars that can be packed in beeswax wraps or in a tin.
- **Do your research**. Check out the increasing number of responsible safari and adventure-holiday tour operators who flag up plastic-free holidays. Many independent hotels have gone a lot further to be plastic-free than some of the big global chains.
- **Plan ahead**. Pack food from home for the journey rather than buying plastic-covered convenience food on the go.

☑ SOLID OR PLASTIC-FREE TOILETRIES

☑ REUSABLE CUTLERY

☑ REUSABLE WATER BOTTLE

☑ REUSABLE SHOPPING BAGS

▲ Take all your eco-essentials with you on holiday to make plastic-free travel a breeze.

Glossary

biodegradable Able to be broken down completely into natural components by bacteria and other organisms.

biodiversity The variety of life forms in a given area and the complex interactions between them.

biomass The total quantity of organisms in an area; also a fuel made of organic material, such as plant matter, food waste, and animal manure.

the carbon cycle The process by which carbon moves between the atmosphere, ocean, and living organisms; see p.208.

carbon dioxide (CO_2) A major component of the carbon cycle; also the main greenhouse gas released into the atmosphere by human activities, including deforestation and burning fossil fuels.

carbon footprint Greenhouse-gas emissions caused, directly or indirectly, by an activity, product, individual, organization, or service.

carbon offsetting The process of coordinating or investing in activities that reduce the amount of carbon in the atmosphere by an amount equivalent to the carbon released by a previous activity.

carbon sink A system that absorbs more carbon from the atmosphere than it emits; the major natural carbon sinks are plants, the ocean, and soil.

climate change Long-term change to the Earth's climate caused by rising average temperatures as a result of human activities, notably the burning of fossil fuels.

CO_2 equivalent (CO_2-eq) A measure of greenhouse-gas emissions calculated by converting all emissions to the equivalent quantities of carbon dioxide.

compostable Able to be broken down into natural components by bacteria and other organisms in specific (compost) conditions and a relatively short time frame.

deforestation The felling of large numbers of trees to clear land, usually for commercial agriculture.

desertification The process by which land in dry areas is irreversibly degraded to a point where it can no longer support plant growth.

dioxins A group of toxic chemical compounds that persist in the environment and accumulate in the food chain.

ecosystem A community of life forms and its physical environment, interconnected by the cycling of nutrients and the flow of energy.

eutrophication Overenrichment of a body of water by nutrients, often from agricultural run-off; effects include excessive growth of algae and deteriorated water quality.

fossil fuel A natural product formed from decayed organic material hundreds of millions of years ago, e.g. crude oil, coal, natural gas; now used by humans as an energy source.

fracking A controversial method of extracting oil or gas by injecting pressurized liquid into rock formations below ground.

genetic modification (GM) The practice of manipulating an organism's genes to give it desired properties, such as resistance to weedkillers in a crop plant.

greenhouse gases Gases that, when present in the atmosphere, trap heat from the sun and warm the planet (a process known as the greenhouse effect). The six greenhouse gases are water vapor, carbon dioxide, methane, nitrous oxide, fluorinated gases, and ozone; these vary in abundance, persistence, and warming effect.

greenwashing Presenting a company's actions as being environmentally beneficial while concealing more damaging actions.

hydrofluorocarbons (HFCs) A group of synthetic chemicals that have commonly been used in refrigeration; they are highly potent and long-lasting greenhouse gases.

methane (CH_4) A greenhouse gas released by natural wetlands and melting permafrost, as well as by fossil-fuel combustion, grazing livestock, decay in landfill, and rice cultivation; it is 25 times more potent than carbon dioxide.

microplastics Small pieces of plastic, less than 5mm in length, which collect in water, soil, and the bodies of animals when larger plastic items break down.

monoculture The practice of cultivating a single crop or livestock species, in particular an agricultural or forest crop, in a given area.

ocean acidification The chemical process by which the water in the oceans absorbs carbon dioxide from the atmosphere and becomes more acidic, impacting species that live in it.

organic Grown without the use of synthetic chemical fertilizers, pesticides, or genetic modification.

ozone (O_3) A gas that forms a layer in the Earth's upper atmosphere, protecting the planet from the Sun's harmful ultraviolet radiation; it also acts as a greenhouse gas and pollutant in the lower atmosphere, where its levels have increased as a result of human activities.

parabens A group of synthetic chemicals often used as preservatives in cosmetics and personal-care products; it has been suggested that they can cause health problems such as disruption of hormone function.

recyclable Able to be broken down and reconstituted to produce new items.

renewable energy Energy from a source with an unlimited or replenishable supply.

volatile organic compounds (VOCs) Certain chemicals that easily evaporate into gases at normal room temperature; many are harmful to health and are emitted from common materials such as paints, adhesives, cleaning products, and building materials.

Bibliography

10 11 years left: © UN: www.un.org/press/en/2019/ga12131.doc.htm. Ice melt data: NASA sealevel.nasa.gov. Increase in global carbon emissions: Ritchie, H. and Roser, M., Our World in Data, ourworldindata.org/co2-emissions. **13** Air pollution risk: © 2019 Health Effects Institute www.stateofglobalair.org/sites/default/files/soga_2019_report.pdf. Truckload of plastic: Fela, J. © Greenpeace International 2020 www.greenpeace.org. **14** 93% of energy imbalance: How fast are the oceans warming? Cheng, L. et al., Science 11 Jan 2019: Vol. 363, Issue 6423: 128–129, doi:10.1126/science.aav7619 © 2019, American Association for the Advancement of Science. Species under threat of extinction: © UN www.un.org/sustainabledevelopment /blog/2019/05/nature-decline-unprecedented-report/. 90% of plastic not recycled: Beeson, L. © University of Georgia, Athens news.uga.edu/royal-statistic-of-2018-90-5-of-plastic-not-recycled/. **21** 9 million refrigerators: United States Environmental Protection Agency, 19january2017snapshot.epa.gov/rad/disposing-appliances-responsibly_.html. **23** Dishwasher stats: Home Water works: © 2011, 2019 Alliance for Water Efficiency, NFP. www.home-water-works.org/ indoor-use/dishwasher. **24** Paper and paperboard recycling data: EPA, United States Environmental Protection Agency: www.epa.gov/facts-and-figures-about-materials-waste-and-recycling/paper-and-paperboard-material-specific-data. Glass bottles and jars recycling data: United States Environmental Protection Agency: www.epa.gov/facts-and-figures-about-materials-waste-and-recycling/glass-material-specific-data. Plastic bottles recycling data: APR: © 2020 The Association of Plastic Recyclers: plasticsrecycling.org/news-and-media/866-december-17-2018-apr-press-release. Aluminium cans recycling data: © 2020 The Aluminum Association www.aluminum.org/aluminum-can-advantage. US 2kg a day: United States Environmental Protection Agency: www.epa.gov/facts-and-figures-about-materials-waste-and-recycling/national-overview-facts-and-figures-materials. **25** Plastic recycled: National Geographic Partners, LLC www.nationalgeographic.com/ news/2017/07/plastic-produced-recycling-waste-ocean-trash-debris-environment/. **26** Food waste graphic data: Department of Communications, Climate Action and Environment: www.dccae.gov.ie/en-ie/environment/topics/sustainable-development/waste-prevention-programme/Pages/Stop-Food-Waste0531-7331.aspx. **27** 4.5 million tonnes of food wasted: © WRAP 2020: wrap.org.uk/sites/files/wrap/Food_%20surplus_and_waste_in_the_UK_key_facts_Jan_2020.pdf. **29** Cotton decomposition Down2Earth Materials: www.down2earthmaterials.ie/2013/02/14/decompose/. **31** 13 billion pounds of paper towels: © 2017 The Energy Co-op web.archive.org/web/20170430185100/www.theenergy.coop/community/blog/ banish-paper-towel. **34** 37% of total GHG emissions: IPCC, 2019: Summary for Policymakers, In: Climate Change and Land: an IPCC special report on climate change, desertification, land degradation, sustainable land management, food security, and greenhouse gas fluxes in terrestrial ecosystems [P.R. Shukla, et al. (eds.)], www.ipcc.ch/srccl/chapter/chapter-5/. Graph data: ERS/USDA http://shrinkthatfootprint/com/food-carbon-footprint-diet. **35** 13 billion eggs: www.egginfo.co.uk/ egg-facts-and-figures/industry-information/data. **36** Carbon footprints of livestock: Ritchie, H., Our World in Data: ourworldindata.org/less-meat-or-sustainable-meat. **38** 1 in 5 Millennials changed diet: © 2018 YouGov PLC: today.yougov. com/topics/food/articles-reports/2020/01/23/millennials-diet-climate-change-environment-poll. **41** Use of soymeal cut by 75%: Food choices, health and environment, Westhoek, H. et al., Global Environmental Change © 2014 The Authors. Published by Elsevier Ltd. doi:10.1016/j.gloenvcha.2014.02.004. **44** 85% of palm oil and 50% of products: WWF UK www. wwf.org.uk/updates/8-things-know-about-palm-oil?gclsrc=aw. **47** Energy efficiency: NCBI, Muller, A. et al. Strategies for feeding the world more sustainably with organic agriculture. Nat Commun, 2017;8(1):1290, doi:10.1038/s41467-017-01410-w. EU target: © European Union, 2020 ec.europa.eu/food/sites/food/files/safety/docs/f2f_action_plan_2020_strategy-info_en.pdf. Graphic inspiration: Reganold, J. and Wachter, J. Organic agriculture in the 21st century, fig.4. Nature Plants. 2, 15221 (2016). doi:10.1038/nplants.2015.221. **48** Tomatoes data: Theurl, M.C. et al. Contrasted GHG emissions from local versus long-range tomato production. Agron. Sustain. Dev. 34, 593–602 (2014) doi:10.1007/s13593-013-0171-8. **54** 75% of food from 12 plants and 5 animal species: © FAO: www.fao.org/3/x0171e/x0171e03.htm. **56** Ultra-processed food: NCBI, Rauber, F. et al., Ultra-Processed Food Consumption and Chronic Non-Communicable Diseases-Related Dietary Nutrient Profile in the UK (2008–2014). Nutrients. 2018;10(5):587. doi:10.3390/nu10050587. 58% of food waste: ©2016 ReFED www.refed.com/downloads/ReFED_Report_2016.pdf. **57** Greenest form of sugar: Hashem, K. et al. (2015) Does sugar pass the environmental and social test? www.researchgate.net. Land occupied by corn in the US: NASS, U.S. Department of Agriculture downloads.usda.library.cornell.edu/usda-esmis/files/j098zb09zvx022244t/8910kf38j/acrg0620.pdf. **59** 40% of US households: Bedford, E. © Statista 2020 www.statista.com/statistics/316217/us-ownership-of-single-cup-brewing-systems/. **60** 2.8 billion coffee cups: Deutsche Umwelthilfe www.duh.de/uploads/tx_duhdownloads/DUH_Coffee-to-go_

Hintergrund_01.pdf. Graph data: © CIRAIG ciraig.org/wp-content/uploads/2020/05/CIRAIG_RapportACVtassesetgobelets_public.pdf. **61** Access to clean water: UN, WHO/UNICEF Joint Monitoring Program (JMP) for Water Supply, Sanitation and Hygiene: www.unwater.org/publications/whounicef-joint-monitoring-program-for-water-supply-sanitation-and-hygiene-jmp-progress-on-household-drinking-water-sanitation-and-hygiene-2000-2017/. 34 billion plastic bottles: Oceana, Inc. oceana.org/press-center/press-releases/oceana-report-soft-drink-industry-can-stop-billions-plastic-bottles. 170l of water: Soda Politics: Taking on Big Soda (And Winning), Nestle, M. **62** France's vineyards: HAL, Aubertot, J-N. et al. Pesticides, agriculture et environnement. Réduire l'utilisation des pesticides et en limiter les impacts environnementaux. 2005. ffhal-02832492f, hal.inrae.fr/hal-02832492/document. **64** 1,000,000 disposable barbecues: Hall, M.,BusinessWaste.co.uk, www.businesswaste.co.uk/disposable-bbqs-should-be-banned-to-prevent-further-devastating-wildfires/. **66** Food waste by restaurants in UK: WRAP, wrap.org.uk/sites/files/wrap/Restaurants.pdf. **68** 75 burgers a second: Guenette R., The Motley Fool © 2020 USA Today, a division of Gannett Satellite Information Network, LLC.www.usatoday.com/story/money/markets/2013/11/19/five-things-about-mcdonalds/3643557/. **72** Water capacity of bath/shower: USGS water.usgs.gov/edu/activity-percapita.php. Length of shower: Hubbub-Trewin Restorick: www.hubbub.org.uk/blog/how-long-do-you-spend-in-the-shower-hubbub-launches-tapchat. **74** Liquid soap vs solid: Comparing the Environmental Footprints of Home-Care Personal-Hygiene Products, Koehler, A. et al., Environ. Sci. Technol. 2009, 43 (22) 8643-8651, doi:10.1021/es901236f © 2009 American Chemical Society. **76** Toilet rolls per capita: Armstrong, M., Statista Consumer Market Outlook www.statista.com/chart/15676/cmo-toilet-paper-consumption/. Bidets in Venezuela: Thomas, J., Treehugger www.treehugger.com/bidets-eliminate-toilet-paper-increase-your-hygiene-4855234. **77** Water use of flushing: © 2019 Waterwise Ltd: waterwise.org.uk/save-water/. **79** Period pants: © 2020 City to Sea www.citytosea.org.uk/campaign/plastic-free-periods/faqs/. **82** Palm oil in 70% of cosmetics: Rai, V., Mint: © HT Digital Streams Limited www.livemint.com/mint-lounge/features/unseen-2019-the-ugly-side-of-beauty-waste-11577446070730.html. **85** 45 million Americans: Centers for Disease Control and Prevention, CDC www.cdc.gov/contactlenses/fast-facts.html. Data for graph: ASU BioDesign Institute, Arizona State University: biodesign.asu.edu/news/first-nationwide-study-shows-environmental-costs-contact-lenses. 39% of contact lenses wearers: Johnson & Johnson Vision Care,Inc.: www.jjvision.com/press-release/johnson-johnson-vision-launches-uks-first-free-nationwide-recycling-programme-all. **87** 1.8 billion cotton buds: © FIDRA www.cottonbudproject.org.uk/plastic-cotton-bud-sticks-in-marine-litter.html. **91** 60 billion sq m of textiles: Chung, S-W. © Greenpeace International 2020: www.greenpeace.org/international/story/7539/fast-fashion-is-drowning-the-world-we-need-a-fashion-revolution/. 90% decrease in Aral sea: The Aral Sea Disaster, Micklin, P., Annual Review of Earth and Planetary Sciences Vol. 35:47-72 (Vol dated 30 May 2007) doi:10.1146/annurev.earth.35.031306.140120. **93** 9 months stat: © WRAP 2020 www.wrap.org.uk/content/extending-life-clothes. **96** Fibre release data: Animashaun, C., Vox © 2020 Vox Media, LLC www.vox.com/the-goods/2018/9/19/17800654/clothes-plastic-pollution-polyester-washing-machine. **98** Laundry stat: Energy Star www.energystar.gov/index.cfm?c=clotheswash.clothes_washers_save_money. Eco-egg data: © ecoegg www.ecoegg.com/product/laundry-egg/. **104** People who need glasses: VisionWatch Eyewear US Study www.thevisioncouncil.org. **105** 50% of gold: Garside, M., © Statista 2020 www.statista.com/statistics/299609/gold-demand-by-industry-sector-share/. Jewellery production by 95%: Pandora Ethics Report pandoragroup.com/-/media/files/pdf/sustainability-reports/pandora_ethics_report_2016.pdf. **110** Pyramid stat: © Sustainable Table sustainabletable.org.au/all-things-ethical-eating/ethical-shopping-pyramid/. **111** 800,000 tonnes of plastic packaging: Eunomia Research & Consulting Ltd 2014 www.eunomia.co.uk/informing-the-plastics-debate/. **112** Bag reuse: © Environment Agency: assets.publishing.service.gov.uk/government/uploads/system/uploads/attachment_data/file/291023/scho0711buan-e-e.pdf. Plastic bags used: © 2013-2020 studylib.net studylib.net/doc/18206586/plastic-bags---worldwatch-institute. Recycling rate: © 2020 TheWorldCounts www.theworldcounts.com/challenges/planet-earth/waste/plastic-bags-used-per-year/story. **113** 40% of shoppers: Clemson University TigerPrints Kimmel, Sc.D. and Robert, M., "Life Cycle Assessment of Grocery Bags in Common Use in the United States" (2014), Environmental Studies. 6, tigerprints.clemson.edu/cudp_environment/6- tigerprints.clemson.edu/cgi/viewcontent.cgi?article=1006&context=cudp_environment. **116** Online shopping graph data: Lipsman, A., eMarkter: © 2020 eMarketer inc. www.emarketer.com/content/global-ecommerce-2019. **118** 40% food wasted: Food and Agriculture Organization of the UN www.fao.org/3/a-bt300e.pdf. **126** 10 million unwanted gifts: ING © Copyright 2018 ING newsroom.ing.com.au/australians-dreaming-of-a-green-christmas/. **127** 227,000 miles wrapping paper: Browning, N., © 2020 Reuters: uk.reuters.com. **128** Commercial shipping emissions: © Copyright 2020 International Maritime Organization (IMO) www.imo.org/en/OurWork/Environment/PollutionPrevention/AirPollution/Pages/Greenhouse-Gas-Studies-2014.aspx. **129** Average CO_2 emissions: © 2020 Carbon Trust: www.carbontrust.com/news-and-events/news/carbon-trust-christmas-tree-disposal-advice. 7 million trees discarded: The Conversation © 2010–2020, The Conversation Media Group Ltd: theconversation.com/new-recycling-process-could-help-your-christmas-tree-lead-a-surprising-second-life-107984. **131** Balloon bits deadly to birds: Roman, L. et al. A quantitative analysis linking seabird mortality and marine debris ingestion, Sci Rep 9, 3202 (2019) doi:10.1038/s41598-018-36585-9. Rubber balloons stats: EPBC © Copyright 2020 European Balloon and Party Council-ebpcouncil.eu/about/balloon-industry. **134** Renewable energy data: Evans, S., Carbon Brief Ltd © 2015 www.carbonbrief.org. **135** Graph data: BP PLC www.bp.com/en/global/corporate/energy-economics/statistical-review-of-world-energy/renewable-energy.html. **136** Energy consumption at home: © Crown copyright 2012 Department of Energy & Climate Change: assets.publishing.service.gov.uk/government/uploads/system/uploads/attachment_data/file/128720/6923-how-much-energy-could-be-saved-by-making-small-cha.pdf. **142** UK expenditure on household appliances: Sabanoglu, T., © Statista 2020 www.statista.com/statistics/301025/annual-expenditure-on-household-appliances-in-the-united-kingdom-uk/. 50 million tonnes of e-waste: UN environment programme © UNEP-www.unenvironment.org/news-and-stories/press-release/un-report-time-seize-opportunity-tackle-challenge-e-waste. **143** Metals in smartphones: © Compound Interest 2014 i1.wp.com/www.compoundchem.com/wp-content/uploads/2014/02/The-Chemical-Elements-of-a-Smartphone-v2.ng?ssl=1. **147** Garden area: The domestic garden: its contribution to urban green infrastructure, Cameron, R. et al. doi:10.1016/j.ufug.2012.01.002. **148** 10% wild bee species: © Friends of the Earth Limited friendsoftheearth.uk/bees/what-are-causes-bee-decline. Over 40% of insect species dying out: © 2019 Elsevier Ltd. Sánchez-Bayo, F. and Wyckhuys, K.A.G. doi:10.1016/j.biocon.2019.01.020. Germany lost 76% of flying insect population: © 2017 Hallmann et al. (2017) More than 75% decline over 27 years in total flying insect biomass in protected areas, PLoS ONE 12(10): e0185809, doi:10.1371/journal.pone.0185809. **151** Carbon sequestration: © United States Forest Service 2008 www.nrs.fs.fed.us/pubs/jrnl/2009/

nrs_2009_pouyat_001.pdf. **154** Properties in England at risk of flooding: © Environment Agency 2009 assets.publishing. service.gov.uk/government/uploads/system/uploads/attachment_data/file/292928/geho0609bqds-e-e.pdf. Concrete industry: Timperley, J., Carbon Brief Ltd © 2015 www.carbonbrief.orgqa-why-cement-emissions-matter-for-climate-change. **160** 150kg of food waste: © WRAP 2020 www.wrap.org.uk/contenthome-composting. **162** Harmful substances in the air: NASA Technical Reports Server ntrs.nasa.gov/citations/19930073077. **166** Lockdown cut energy-related emissions: Darby, M., © 2020 Climate Home News Ltd.- www.climatechangenews.com/2020/05/19/coronavirus-lockdown-cut-energy-related-co2-emissions-17-study-finds/. **167** Disposable coffee cups: Bell, S. © 2019 RoadRunner Recycling Inc. www.roadrunnerwm .com/blog/office-worker-waste-generation. **168** Data centre data: © 2018 Super Micro Computer, Inc. www.supermicro. com/wekeepitgreen/Data_Centers_and_the_Environment_Dec2018_Final.pdf. Energy consumption by data centres: Vidal, J. © 2020 Climate Home News Ltd: www.climatechangenews.com/2017/12/11/tsunami-data-consume-one-fifth-global-electricity-2025/. **169** CO_2-e emissions graph data: © Copyright 2018 Environmental Paper Network: environmentalpaper. org/wp-content/uploads/2018/04StateOfTheGlobalPaperIndustry2018_FullReport-Final.pdf. **170** 4% of global carbon emissions: The Think Tank The Shift Project theshiftproject.org/wp-contentuploads/2019/03Lean-ICT-Report_The-Shift-Project_2019.pdf. **171** Global emails sent: Clement, J. © Statista 2020 www.statista.com. Graphic data: Berners-Lee, M., How Bad are Bananas?: The Carbon Footprint of Everything, 2010. Extra 7 million cars: © Immediate Media Company Ltd 2020 www.sciencefocus.com/planet-earth/. One less email a day: OVO Energy www.ovoenergy.com/ovo-newsroom/ press-releases/2019/november/think-before-you-thank-if-every-brit-sent-one-less-thank-you-email-a-day-we-would-save-16433-tonnes-of-carbon-a-year-the-same-as-81152-flights-to-madrid.html. 60% of internet use: © 2020 Sandvine www. sandvine.com/hubfs/Sandvine_Redesign_2019/Downloads/2020/Phenomena/COVID%20Internet%20Phenomena%20 Report%2020200507.pdf. **172** Average book 7.46kg of CO_2 and e-books data: © 2002–2009 Cleantech Group LLC. gato-docs.its.txstate.edu/jcr:4646e321-9a29-41e5-880d-4c5ffe69e03e/thoughts_ereaders.pdf. **173** 374 million magazines: Johnson, J. © Statista 2020 www.statista.com/statistics/322476/magazine-print-sales-volume-uk/. 85% of global news revenues: © 2020 WAN-IFRA World Association of News Publishers www.wan-ifra.org/reports/2019/10/28/world-press-trends-2019. **175** Socially responsible investing growth: Triodos Bank UK Ltd www.triodos.co.uk/press-releases/2018/ socially-responsible-investing-market-on-cusp-of-momentus-growth. Investing increased by 34%: The Global Sustainable Investment Alliance www.gsi-alliance.org/wp-content/uploads/2019/03/GSIR_Review2018.3.28.pdf. **180** 565 condoms: The Associated Press apnews.com/article/23c459322ab24a86b458e71615784e42. **183** More than 65% of women use lube: © 2014 International Society for Sexual Medicine, Women's Use and Perceptions of Commercial Lubricants, Herbenick, D. et al., doi:10.1111/jsm.1242. **184** CO_2 generation data: Ritchie, H., Our World in Data: ourworldindata.org/per-capita-co2. Land mammals lost habitat: © 2020 National Academy of Sciences, Population losses and the 6th mass extinction, Ceballos, G. et al. PNAS 25 July 2017 114 (30) E6089-E6096; doi:10.1073/pnas.1704949114. **185** 58.6 tonnes CO_2: © 2017 IOP Publishing Ltd, The climate mitigation gap, Wynes, S. and Nicholas, K.A. 2017 Environ. Res. Lett. 12 074024, doi:10.1088/ 1748-9326/aa7541. 40,000 children seek new homes: © Copyright 2020 Adopt Change www.adoptchange.org.au/page/38/ the-issue. Number of nappies used: © WRAP 2020 www.wrap.org.uk/content/real-nappies-overview. Reusable vs disposable nappies: © Environment Agency assets.publishing.service.gov.uk/government/uploads/system/uploads/ attachment_data/file/291130/scho0808boir-e-e.pdf. **187** 85% of babies: © 2020 Advameg, Inc. www.healthofchildren. com/P/Pacifier-Use.html. **190** Domestic cats data: Trouwborst, A. and Somsen, H., Domestic Cats (Felis catus) and European Nature Conservation Law, Journal of Environ. Law, eqz035 doi:10.1093/jel/eqz035. 64 million tonnes of CO_2 from pets: © 2017 Okin, G.S. (2017).Environmental impacts of food consumption by dogs and cats, PLoS ONE 12(8):doi: 10.1371/journal.pone.0181301. Cats killing birds: © The Royal Society for the Protection of Birds (RSPB) www.rspb.org.uk. 67% US households: ©1998–2020 American Pet Products Association, Inc. www.americanpetproducts.org/pubs.survey. asp. **192** 25% of resources: © 2017 Okin, G.S. Graphic stat: © Mars 2019 www.royalcanin.com/au/about-us/news/ new-survey-weighs-up-potential-reasons-behind-the-pet-obesity-crisis. **194** Americans choosing cremation: ©2020 by National Funeral Directors Association nfda.org/news/statistics. **195** Graphic data: Coutts, C. et al., Natural burial as a land conservation tool in the US, doi:10.1016/j.landurbplan.2018.05.022. **198** 14% of total emissions: © Intergovernmental Panel on Climate Change 2014 www.ipcc.ch/site/assets/uploads/2018/02/ipcc_wg3_ar5_full.pdf. Buses CO_2: Carbon Independent, www.carbonindependent.com/20.html. Graphic data: ©IEA 2020 web.archive.org/web/20200103091659if_/ https://www.iea.org/reports/tracking-transport-2019. **201** 60% of people: Schaller Consulting www.schallerconsult.com/ rideservices/automobility.htm. Emissions of electric vehicle cut by 73%: European Environment Agency www.eea. europa.eu/highlights/eea-report-confirms-electric-cars. 10% of people in UK: Wagner, I., Statista Inc www.statista.com/ topics/2298/the-uk-electric-vehicle-industry/. Electric car emissions: © 2020 International Council on Clean Transportation. theicct.org/publications/EV-battery-manufacturing-emissions. Making electric cars vs petrol CO_2: © Copyright 2020 Ricardo ricardo.com/news-and-media/news-and-press/ricardo-study-demonstrates-importance-of-whole-lif. Idling: © 2020 Environmental Defense Fund www.edf.org. **203** Speeds below 55mph: © Copyright 2018 Norcom Insurance www. norcominsurance.com/windows-down-vs-ac-which-is-more-fuel-efficient/. 250kg CO_2 data: Carbon Independent.org www. carbonindependent.org/22.html. Fuel economy reduction: Huff, S. et al., "Effects of Air Conditioner Use on Real-World Fuel Economy", SAE Technical Paper, 2013, doi:10.4271/2013-01-0551. **207** Number of Flights in 2019: Mazareanu, E., Statista Inc: www.statista.com/statistics/564769/airline-industry-number-of-flights/#statisticContainer. Airport Emissions data: Jung, Y., NASA Ames Research Center: flight.nasa.gov/pdf/18_jung_green_aviation_summit.pdf. 15% of UK population took 70% of flights: Department of Transport assets.publishing.service.gov.uk/government/uploads/system/uploads/attachment_ data/file/336702/experiences-of-attitudes-towards-air-travel.pdf. **209** 140-fold growth: Forest Trends, Voluntary Carbon Markets Insights www.forest-trends.org/wp-content/uploads/2019/04/VCM-Q1-Report-Final.pdf. **211** 1.4 billion people on holiday: World Tourism Organization (2019), International Tourism Highlights, 2019 Edition, UNWTO, Madrid, doi:10.18111/9789284421152. **212** People wanting to travel sustainably: © 1996–2020 Booking.com B.V. globalnews. booking.com/where-sustainable-travel-is-headed-in-2018/

For further sources visit

www.dk.com/iirg-biblio

Index

About the author

Georgina Wilson-Powell is a journalist and the founder and editor of pebble, an online sustainable lifestyle magazine that provides news, features, and reviews on issues from ethical fashion to eco-travel, plastic-free developments to permaculture (www.pebblemag.com). pebble also has an online community and organises online and offline eco-festivals. Georgina also acts as a consultant on sustainable issues and editorial strategy to corporations and charities, and has been a magazine publisher and editor for 17 years, working for Time Out, BBC Good Food, and Lonely Planet Traveller. She now lives in Margate with her partner and dog.

Acknowledgments

Author's acknowledgments
Thanks to Beth for never-ending support, to my mum for instilling in me that being a journalist and author is the best thing you can be, and to Martin, without whom there would have been no pebble and no journey into a vast environmental education or urgency to act.

Thanks to the team at DK for throwing themselves into creating one of the most sustainable books ever and for being keen to help change the consumer game.

For every eco-activist, keen armchair warrior, placard-waving protestor, hopeful campaigner, and worried parent. We can do this when we act together. Start now.

Publisher's acknowledgments
We would like to acknowledge the help of the following in the production of this book: Kiron Gill for editorial assistance; Alethea Doran for proofreading; Marie Lorimer for providing the index; Francesca Sturiale, Nicola Torode, Lindsey Scott, and Luca Bazzoli for helping to make the production process for this book as green as possible.

All images © Dorling Kindersley
For more information visit
www.dk.com